SHERRY SCHILLER, Ph.D.

DISPELLING THE MEGATRENDS MYTH:
A LEADER'S GUIDE TO MANAGING CHANGE

THE SCHILLER CENTER   Alexandria, Virginia

Copyright 1994 The Schiller Center

All rights reserved. No part of this book
may be reproduced in any form
or by any means without written permission
from the publisher.

Library of Congress Catalog Card Number 94-092143

Edited by Sharon Block
Designed by Stephen Kraft
Printed by Custom Print, Inc.
   Arlington, Virginia

ISBN 0-9641259-0-0

Dedicated to my mom and dad,
whose philosophy has always been,
"Forward ever, backward never."

Contents

	FOREWORD	9
	INTRODUCTION	11
	SECTION I: Beyond Megatrends	14
MYTH #1	The Future Is Determined Primarily by Forces Beyond Our Control.	15
CHAPTER ONE	An Open, Undetermined Future	16
TWO	Possibilities: Expanding Horizons	22
THREE	Probabilities: Megatrends — *Nega*trends	25
FOUR	Preferabilities: Guiding Visions	31
FIVE	Four Futures Formulas	35
	SECTION II: The Nature of Contemporary Change	42
MYTH #2	We Cannot Understand the Nature of Contemporary Change.	43
CHAPTER SIX	The Characteristics of Contemporary Change	45
SEVEN	The Form-Driven Paradigm of the Past	51
EIGHT	A Function-Driven Paradigm for the Future	61
NINE	Styles of Managing Change	70
	SECTION III: Managing Change: The 21st-Century Leadership Challenge	80
MYTH #3	There Is Nothing We Can Do to Influence the Future.	81
CHAPTER TEN	Building a Long-Term, Global Perspective	83
ELEVEN	Concentrating on Quality	93

TWELVE	Encouraging Innovation	102
THIRTEEN	Improving Cooperation and Communication	109
FOURTEEN	Committing to Ethical Practices	115
FIFTEEN	Exercising Empowerment	125
SIXTEEN	Being Propelled by Purpose	130
	PERSONAL/ORGANIZATIONAL INVENTORY	143
	ABOUT THE AUTHOR	150

Foreword

The belief that the future is determined by forces outside of our control is a dangerous one. It causes us to act in ways that reinforce that notion, lending credence to it. When we believe we do not make a difference, we don't bother voting. "What difference does my vote make, anyway?" we reason. We live with injustices in our communities and inequities in our workplaces because we conclude, "That's just the way it is." We set our sights low for ourselves, our families, our organizations, and our nation. We focus on what we can get, not on what we can give, because we have already convinced ourselves that giving doesn't really change anything.

The truly great people I have known in my life have never accepted the notion that the future was beyond their grasp. Whether they were world leaders or everyday citizens, they had a vision of how things could be better and worked to achieve that vision.

My wife Margaret was the most remarkable example of how this perspective colors everything we do. When I was serving in the Kennedy Administration, President Kennedy called his Cabinet members and their wives into his office early in his term. He suggested to our spouses that they find meaningful contributions to make, as their partners would be working long, hard hours. Margaret had been a teacher and had always cared about education issues, so she searched for a way that she could help young people in the poorer neighborhoods of Washington, D.C. She was appalled to discover as she visited them that many of their homes did not contain a single piece of reading material. Not a book. Not a magazine. Not a newspaper. Nothing.

Margaret realized that these young people's teachers were struggling to get them to read in an environment where there was no foundation for reading. It was no wonder they were falling farther and farther behind in their reading as they grew up. And Margaret knew, of course, that without the ability to read, their futures were severely limited. So what she did was start a program to bring reading materials into their homes and their lives. Out of this volunteer effort grew Reading Is Fundamental, which had over 70,000 volunteers when she died.

This is what believing you can make a difference is all about. It doesn't matter if you are the head of a nation or the head of a household, the same principle applies. If you believe you can make a difference, you will try to do so, and will succeed beyond anything you might have accomplished if you had held a more passive view.

Believing each person can make a difference is the most important first step anyone can take in shaping a positive future. But today something more is required. We must understand the nature of contemporary change and appreciate that it calls for fresh approaches to solving problems. The old mindsets will not produce lasting solutions to today's complex, interconnected issues. And we need to redefine leadership in a 21st century-context.

Dr. Sherry Schiller understands that we need to challenge our old assumptions about the future, about change, and about leadership. In this book she provides a positive framework for managing our entering into that future. Make no mistake: as Dr. Schiller demonstrates, the future is in the hands of each and every one of us.

Robert McNamara
February 1994

Introduction

How many of us recall the enthusiasm and optimism that we brought to our first work experiences? And how many of us have found ourselves over the years expecting less and less of ourselves, our colleagues, and our organizations? Perhaps norms that encourage mediocrity, conformity, and obedience were adequate for the assembly-line organizations of the Industrial Age. Today, they are no longer appropriate.

Now, we need organizations that promote new behaviors that are more appropriate for our fast-paced, global, information-based world. Yet too many of our institutions continue to promote outdated attitudes and behaviors that prevent people from being effective in shaping the future for themselves, their organizations, and their communities.

While assisting business, government, and nonprofit leaders in managing change and preparing for the future, I have observed that those who cling to old assumptions about the future, change, and leadership are doomed to failure regardless of what management trends and techniques they may try to employ. These leaders become frustrated with their inability to get their organizations and their employees to behave the way they want them to. And, of course, a disturbing number of their employees are unhappy in their work. They feel trapped, believing their fate is controlled by their employers.

Too often they do what they are told, never challenging the assumptions, direction, or effectiveness of the orders they receive.

This belief that our future is beyond our own influence is not just a workplace phenomenon. Many of us have given up responsibility for some of the most fundamental decisions in our personal lives. We point to parents, children, spouses, and friends and hold them responsible for what we have failed to achieve.

Even organizations have relinquished control of their destinies. Public institutions, private corporations, and political parties blame outside forces for their difficulties. Leaders in the arts blame their plight on unsympathetic politicians. Educators allow their agendas to be set by business and political figures and then complain that they are powerless. Corporations blame their boards, their managers, federal regulators, or foreign competitors, and government leaders blame one another.

The tendency to deny responsibility has been reinforced by the widely accepted belief that the future is determined primarily by megatrends — large-scale patterns set in motion by current and past events. Futurists and forecasters who have promoted the megatrends view of the future have contributed to the false impression that the future is shaped not by the actions of individuals but by forces outside of our control. Whether intentionally or inadvertently, they have fostered the myth that only they can understand and interpret such forces for the rest of us. And all too often, we are happy to turn the future over to them.

I have shared my framework for managing change with thousands of people in the United States and abroad. I have conducted hundreds of skill-building workshops on the leadership behaviors for the 21st century. One of the most frequent comments I hear is that my message is clear, practical, and empowering, but that people wish they had *more.* They often say, "I wish I had your presentation on videotape to show my boss and coworkers who couldn't be here." Or, "I'd love to be able to share your ideas with my family so we could discuss them together." Or they say, "I wish I could write your philosophy down and have time to reflect on its implications for my life." This book is an attempt to respond to those requests. It is not a research or academic treatise. Written for people who are trying to cope with change, it is an effort to describe, clearly and succinctly, an approach to the future, change, and leadership that is both powerful and useful.

The time has come to replace old values and behaviors that make us victims of forces beyond our control. The more we give up responsibility for our future, the more we ensure our impotence. The optimism, trust, and sense of unlimited potential that we felt at our first day of school, our first job, and in our first romantic relationship are natural feelings that can be recaptured and harnessed if we empower ourselves and others to shape the future.

There is no room for cynicism or pessimism. If we are going to thrive — if we are even to *survive* — in the 21st century, we must accept responsibility for effectively managing change. The future — *our* future — rests in our hands.

Beyond Megatrends

MYTH #1: **The Future Is Determined Primarily by Forces Beyond Our Control.**

There is a widely held notion that the future is shaped primarily by large-scale forces beyond our control. We have come to accept the megatrends myth that only experts who study the future can identify these large-scale trends. If we allow ourselves to believe that important issues are settled by outside forces and other people, we may conclude that there is little we can do to shape our personal, professional, civic, and global destinies.

How can this megatrends myth be overcome? How can we build a more balanced, proactive view of the future? This section provides a framework for understanding how the future is determined. It places trends alongside other factors shaping the future. It emphasizes the role that human choice plays in shaping the future.

Many of our actions are influenced by our beliefs about the future. This section also explores the different, often unconscious, views that people and organizations hold toward the future and how these views affect our behavior.

CHAPTER ONE

An Open, Undetermined Future

"Think of how President John F. Kennedy's assassination *changed history,*" said someone I recently met at a professional conference. "Yes, and the tragic loss of Dr. Martin Luther King, Jr.," added another member of our group. "What about the landing on the moon as a positive event that *altered the future?*" offered a third. In our culture, such references to changing history or altering the future are commonplace. They are signs of a widely held belief that the future already exists. Many people assume that the future is set, alterable only by dramatic, earth-shattering events.

This view was reinforced in the 1980s by the popular megatrends concept that certain experts can identify large-scale trends as the primary forces that shape the future. First made popular by John Naisbitt's 1982 book *Megatrends,* the megatrends message led people to conclude that large-scale patterns *were* the future and that we could do little to influence what was to come.

The megatrends message fit with the generally accepted view of the future as singular and preestablished. Most of us think of the relationship between the past, present, and future as a continuum. We believe that there was *one past,* there is *one present,* and that there will be *one future.* We conclude that a single, predetermined future exists somewhere "out there" — waiting its turn to become the present.

This belief is most clearly exhibited by those in our society who turn to futurists, astrologers, forecasters, clairvoyants, palm readers, and prophets — "special individuals" who are believed to be capable of revealing what the future holds. This view is shared in a more subtle way by thousands of individuals, organizations, and cultures who assume that trends, God, or destiny has already mapped out a course for them.

Common View of the Future:

past   present   future

The belief that the future is singular and preexistent is both inaccurate and unproductive. When we believe the future is essentially set by forces outside of our control, we conclude that we can do nothing to affect it, and we have little motivation to try. Naturally, the less we try to influence the future, the less influence we have, which in turn reinforces our conviction that the future is beyond our grasp. This cycle creates a negative self-fulfilling prophesy.

Assumptions that the future is preset and beyond our influence have a powerful impact on how we live our lives. For example, I worked with a person who habitually complained that she would never attain her dream job, home, or car with her limited education and experience. She was sure as well that further education was not possible for her. She felt trapped in every aspect of her life, convinced that she was the victim of forces she could never overcome. She remained in an unhealthy relationship, believing that her "die was cast" and that nothing could turn her life around. Because she could only read one script for how her life would unfold and felt powerless to rewrite that script, she accepted her "destiny," unable to recognize assets and opportunities that others might have seized.

Organizations likewise get locked into viewing the future as predetermined and out of their control. Many leaders wrongly conclude that their organizations can only continue to follow patterns set in the past and that these patterns are determined by forces beyond their influence. They are convinced that, even if they try to react to large-scale events affecting their organizations, the future depends primarily on forces they have trouble comprehending, let alone controlling. A manufacturing firm I worked with fell prey to this thinking when the industry in which the firm was active faced inroads from foreign competition at the same time it faced new legislation requiring greater environmental responsibility. Rather than look for opportunities presented by these challenges, the firm's executives threw their hands up in despair and blamed their foreign competitors and the U.S. Congress. As their business eroded, they complained to their stockholders that they were victims of outside forces and could do nothing but lay off employees, close factories, and drop product lines.

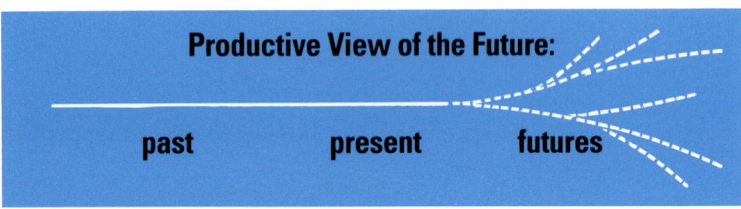

As I worked with the leaders of this organization, they began to view the future as theirs to shape and their actions changed. Today, they have carved out a very profitable niche in their industry — producing high-end goods that are manufactured in an environmentally friendly manner.

In fact, there is no single, predetermined future. We cannot "change" the future because it does not yet exist. Indeed, an unlimited number of alternative futures is open to us beyond the present. The number of alternative futures is limited only by our imagination and ability to invent them.

If we move beyond blindly accepting the future as a single, predetermined course of events that we cannot influence, our minds are free to explore a wide range of alternative futures.

A way to explore alternative futures is in terms of what I call the three P's: **Possibilities, Probabilities, and Preferabilities.**

Possibilities

Possibilities are alternative future options. The greater the range and number of possibilities identified, the better sense we have of what the future can hold and the wiser choices we can make. When identifying possibilities, it is essential not to be constrained by what seems likely. If a possibility is never identified in the first place, it can never be considered for the likelihood (probability) or desirability (preferability) of it occurring. Nor can it be factored into planning for future contingencies. Because of the uncertainty and volatility of today's world, "unlikely" possibilities occur with great frequency. Therefore, considering the broadest range of possibilities is the best initial step that anyone can take in planning for the future.

A friend of mine from a strong Irish-Catholic family said that when she was growing up, the girls in her family — indeed the girls in families throughout her close-knit ethnic neighborhood — believed they had only two possible futures: to marry and become mothers or to join the convent and become sisters. She said that they never even considered other possibilities. Their life choices were therefore strictly limited. By not exploring other possibilities, these young women limited themselves to a narrow range of options set for them by others.

Similarly, organizations often rush into strategic planning, decision making, and problem solving constricted by a narrow range of possibilities. This practice almost always produces negative results. Limiting options, intentionally or unintentionally, invariably leads to poor decisions. When there are few options from which to select, the best solutions are often left undiscovered and therefore unattained.

In today's complex, interconnected world, decision making is greatly strengthened by considering a wider range of possibilities. In slower-paced times, traditional solutions might have been appropriate for the future. Today, the solutions of the past are often inadequate. Viewing the future as open and composed of many alternatives allows us to generate many fresh solutions to the complex issues we face.

Probabilities

Among all of the possibilities we can identify, some seem more likely to occur than others. These can be called probabilities. Of the three P's, probabilities are the most familiar to us, especially since the popularity of the megatrends message of the 1980s.

Forecasters and futurists have led many of us to conclude that probabilities and possibilities are one and the same. They are not. Too often we erroneously assume that those events deemed "most likely" by some expert are the only ones possible. This can lead us to being unprepared in the likely event that the unlikely should occur. Even educated and powerful leaders incorrectly conclude that the future is composed primarily of probable events. They confuse probabilities with possibilities, unaware that in the future anything is possible but not every possibility is probable. Like many of us, they fail to recognize that the range of probabilities is narrower than the range of possibilities.

Probabilities are patterns from the past projected into the future. When trends are presented as megatrends, they can mistakenly be viewed as a critical mass of unstoppable forces determining the future in an unalterable fashion.

The importance of probabilities or trends has thus been overstated. Yet probabilities can be useful in setting and attaining goals. Knowing what we or others expect to happen can help us define our goals, identify how we will attain them, and determine how hard we may have to work to realize them. We must, however, use trends to achieve our goals, not replace them.

Preferabilities

Preferabilities are desirable alternative futures. Preferabilities are visions of what we want the future to be like. They may be visions for ourselves, our organizations, our communities, or the world. They are based on our values and beliefs, our hopes and dreams.

Preferabilities have been overlooked by many contemporary American futurists, who have been more comfortable addressing probable large-scale trends. If futurists have intentionally ignored values and goals in an effort to be scientific and value-free, they have failed, for their personal biases undergird their work no matter how objectively they may try to present it. At a recent conference of futurists, I was amused to hear experts on a panel quoting the same body of research and reaching contradictory conclusions — all the time arguing vehemently that their findings were "scientifically sound" while those of the other panelists were subjective and inaccurate. Perhaps objectivity is, indeed, in the eye of the beholder.

Earlier in the century, futurists, philosophers, and thinkers understood that preferabilities are more important in achieving goals than are probabilities. During the Nazi occupation of France, French thinkers began to consider that a time of little external freedom could be a time of great internal freedom. Because their country existed only in their minds, they could make it anything they wanted it to be. Following World War II, French philosophers and futurists like Jean Paul Sartre and Bertrand de Jouvenal asked people to consider what they wanted their nation and the world to be like. Similarly, in the 1970s Alvin Toffler asked people to discuss the question, "What kind of world do you want 10, 20, or 30 years from now?"

Preferabilities need to be at the center of all planning. For example, a small professional association I assisted generated five possible scenarios for their future. They determined the likelihood of each, concluding that only two were probable if they continued to operate as they were. They then took an important step — they used this information to decide what they wanted for their future, since the two probable scenarios were not the most preferable ones.

The key to good planning lies in identifying preferabilities — and not just the preferabilities of a few. Planning must take into account the values and goals of everyone who has a stake in the plan. For example, a large nonprofit organization recently found that its strategic-planning effort had come to a standstill. Staff members had become convinced that the trustees had a vision for the organization that was at odds with their own, but because all their planning meetings had focused on trends and what the experts said would *be* rather than their goals and what they thought *should be,* no one knew what anyone else wanted for the organization. Only when all participants openly discussed their visions and goals for the organization — their preferabilities — were they finally able to make progress. In fact, they discovered that staff and trustees shared remarkably compatible visions, which provided a solid foundation on which to build their strategic plans.

Fortunately for us, throughout history many leaders did not accept that the future is a predetermined extension of the past. There have always been people like Marian Wright Edelman, Cesar Chavez, Harriet Tubman, Marie Curie, Jonas Salk, Margaret Sanger, Lech Walensa, and Nelson Mandela, as well as thousands of forgotten discoverers, scientists, thinkers, and activists who believed that the future could be different — different from the past and present, different from the views shared by their contemporaries, and different as a result of their personal influence.

Every day, people accomplish amazing things — things others have described as improbable or even impossible. Many of these individuals are not famous, yet they are heroes in their own right, for they are not bound by the narrow views of others but are guided by their visions of what can be. The more determined we are to accomplish a goal — and the more time and energy we put into it — the greater our chance of achieving it and shaping the future.

CHAPTER TWO

Possibilities: Expanding Horizons

*B*eing able to apply possibilities, probabilities, and preferabilities to planning and decision making is critical to success. In this and the following two chapters, we take a more in-depth look at each of these ways of exploring alternative futures.

Individuals who have had a great impact on shaping the future — people like Harriet Beecher Stowe, the Wright brothers, Albert Einstein, and Winston Churchill — were not limited by the narrow range of possibilities accepted by their contemporaries. They stretched traditional boundaries and saw a world of greater possibilities. They all acted on their belief that, in the future, *anything is possible*. Most of the people we respect in our personal and professional lives share this belief. Like them, all of us can expand our horizons and increase our options by considering a broader range of possibilities. As individuals, organizations, communities, and nations, we can break away from past limitations by expanding the number of possible alternative futures we recognize.

Many of us have difficulty generating a wide range of possibilities. Sometimes we limit our options because we feel overwhelmed, sometimes because we are intellectually lazy, more often because we have no framework for understanding the future. Whatever the cause, too many of us hinder our decision-making ability by considering only a narrow band of familiar options.

Imagination is more important than knowledge.
ALBERT EINSTEIN

Creativity can be described as letting go of certainties.
GAIL SHEEHY

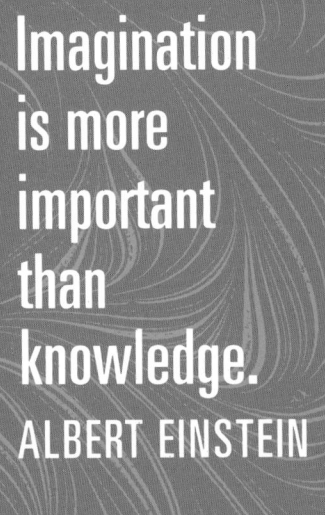

Children, less bound by the self-imposed inhibitions of their elders, enjoy creating numerous imaginative possibilities. In a problem-solving exercise widely used in training and educational settings, most adult teams, when coached, identify three to eight possible solutions to the problem. With the same rules and time restrictions — and no coaching — most teams of 13-year-olds easily generate more than 50! In highly successful brainstorming sessions, corporate leaders have even turned to groups of middle-school students to help them identify fresh solutions to business problems.

Adults, regardless of their profession or education, can have difficulty exploring a wide range of possibilities. We are often content to identify only one or two options for any choice we are considering, regardless of its importance. In team situations, if one member wants to explore additional possibilities, others often disapprove and complain that their time is being wasted.

Retaining the capacity to see possibilities into adulthood can make the difference between success and failure. Charles Goodyear was able to think up 32,000 uses for rubber. He succeeded where others failed because he could see the possibilities in those new situations or products. Western Union, for example, turned down exclusive rights to the telephone in 1878 when its president concluded, "What use could this company make of an electrical toy?"

Many leaders of organizations are not encouraged to consider a wide range of possibilities. Supposedly in an effort to save the leaders' time, their advisors present them with only the most likely scenarios, believing these to be the only ones worth considering. Unfortunately, too many organizations suffer from these self-imposed limitations and are often caught unprepared by a turn of events they had not foreseen.

Organizations and individuals who have considered a wider range of possibilities are much better prepared to handle whatever might occur than are those who build their future on a single probability. A large manufacturing corporation that encouraged its managers to engage in "what if" thinking found that this technique improved both productivity and employee morale. Managers began asking questions like, "What if the mills went down today? What are all the things that could happen? What are all the possible steps we could take to prevent this from occurring? What are all the ways a new federal policy on import tariffs could affect us? What kinds of actions might we take? What could the spin-offs of each one be? What are all the possible uses we could find for the waste generated by Plant Number 21? Are there any that could make us money and be environmentally sound?" Through this simple technique, these managers learned to consider a broader range of possibilities, place problems and opportunities in a wider context, become creative problem solvers, and build contingency plans. And they became team players who developed a personal stake in the future of the company.

Exploring a wide range of possibilities leads not only to better decisions, but also to faster ones. The practice of identifying a wide range of alternatives allows decision makers to spot opportunities and execute their plans before others do. And in today's highly competitive market, the organization or individual who acts first will often be the one who profits most.

Being able to imagine possible future events allows us to prepare for them. Called *contingency planning,* this process begins with generating a wide range of future possibilities so that plans can be constructed to monitor or manage them. Contingency planning often focuses on reducing the undesirable consequences of various possibilities. Critics claim that contingency planning encourages living in the future and focuses on the negative. In truth, preparing a plan for any conceivable turn of events allows us to be more comfortable in the present because we are less worried about the uncertainties of the future. Knowing that we are ready for any possibility that might develop, we feel free to enjoy our lives as they unfold.

Exploring future possibilities also promotes personal and organizational growth. When we explore possibilities, we become more adept at testing our own assumptions. We are less inclined to be driven by our negative biases and obsolete perspectives — and less likely to be the victims of others'. We do not wait for experts to tell us what the future will be. We become better able to monitor and interpret emerging patterns for ourselves. We are able to place them in a context of factors shaping the future without succumbing to the notion that these patterns *are* the future. We feel secure in posing questions to which there are no ready answers. We become more skilled at evaluating the opinions and recommendations of experts. Our thinking becomes more flexible. We improve our ability to respond to unfamiliar or unexpected situations. Considering a full range of possible alternative futures provides an important advantage in managing change in our personal and professional lives and, in a larger sense, on a national and global level.

CHAPTER THREE

Probabilities: Megatrends – *Nega*trends

Alternative futures can also be examined in terms of their probability. Most people are familiar with probabilities because forecasts about everything from football victories to stock market developments have become such an integral part of contemporary life.

All possible future events can be assigned a degree of likelihood, just as weather forecasters predict "a 40 percent chance of rain by midnight" or "a 60 percent chance of snow by the weekend." As with weather forecasting, the accuracy of other forecasts varies greatly and depends on many factors, such as the skill and biases of the forecaster, the quality of the data used, the forecasting techniques, and the extent to which future conditions are likely to be the same as those of the past.

Examining the probability of a future occurrence can be useful in making wiser choices about how to attain one's goals. However, the value of forecasting probable alternative futures has been grossly overstated in the last decade. It is unfortunate that many contemporary American futurists, by focusing on megatrends that they deem "probable," have paid little or no attention to possible and preferable futures. They identify patterns from the past and present, label them "megatrends," and project them into the future as virtual certainties.

The recent fixation with megatrends is misguided at best and harmful at worst. First of all, the accuracy of any forecast depends on past conditions continuing into the future. In very stable, slowly changing times, forecasting can be relatively reliable. Centuries ago, predictions about where the herds of buffalo might congregate or when the crops should be harvested could be handed down from one generation to the next with little need for alteration. So imperceptibly did the conditions of life change from generation to generation that forecasting had a *distant horizon.* People could look far ahead and see conditions very much like those of the present and past. This allowed them to draw fairly reliable conclusions about what would likely occur.

Yet even long ago, when the rate of change was much slower, chance played a role in shaping the future. Forecasters of the past still faced many unforeseen events that made forecasting difficult. An unexpected stampede could cause the buffalo to follow a path they had never taken before, or an unanticipated drought might delay harvesting. The future, even for those whose lives changed little from one generation to the next, still contained an element of uncertainty.

Because of the uncertainties that the future has always held, the experts have often been the last to see the possibilities for change. Tied to the way things have always been, they have frequently been unable to recognize how conditions might be different in the future than the way they have been in the past. Thomas Tredgold, British railroad designer, said with great authority in 1835, "Any general system of conveying passengers... at a velocity exceeding 10 miles per hour, or thereabouts, is extremely improbable." In 1939 *The New York Times* reported, "The problem with television is that the people must sit and keep their eyes glued on the screen; the average American family hasn't time for it.... television will never be a serious competitor for radio." Dr. Richard van der Riet Woolley, Britain's Astronomer Royal, concluded some years after President Dwight D. Eisenhower announced the U.S. Satellite Program, "Space travel is utter bilge." History is filled with the forecasts of experts who were simply wrong about the future.

Forecasters of the past have in fact been more accurate in forecasting new technologies than in forecasting the effects of these innovations on economics, politics, and society as a whole. George Wise, of the General Electric Research and Development Center at Schenectady, New York, compiled a list of 1,556 predictions that had been made publicly by Americans during the half century between 1890 and 1940. Using baseball batting averages as his model, he worked out these forecasters' batting averages by dividing the number of correct predictions by the total number of predictions made. He found that the forecasters' batting average for predicting changes in technology itself was a whopping .420. But their average for forecasting the social, economic, and political implications of these technological advances was a sorry .253! One typical bases-loaded strikeout was Cleveland Moffett's 1900 forecast for automobiles. In *Review of Reviews,* he suggested, "We shall probably find public taste changing so that many people will prefer to travel from place to place more slowly than at present."

When experts can be so wrong in slower changing times, is it any wonder that they so frequently miss the mark in today's tumultuous world? As Yogi Berra said, "The future ain't what it used to be." We cannot count on the future as a logical extension of the past and present. The horizon for accurate predictions has moved in so close that trying to focus on it can make us cross-eyed.

Today's world is fast-paced and discontinuous. Every day brings developments that experts did not foresee. When the Berlin Wall crumbled, the experts admitted that they never thought they would see it happen. But that did not prevent them from insisting that, in any event, East and West Germany would never reunite. Of course, they were proven wrong within months. Similarly, experts were caught off guard by the breakup of the Soviet Union, the dissolution of communism, the unification of South Africa, and a host of other events of global significance.

Another reason for reexamining megatrend mania is that some forecasters intentionally mystify the future rather than clarify it. They promote the belief that decoding the future (i.e., identifying and tracking trends) is a complicated task — certainly not one that lay people should attempt. They encourage the belief that only *they* have access to appropriate data (which, in fact, are widely available) and only *they* have the skills and training to analyze and understand it.

The exploitive nature of these contemporary megatrend maestros is not new. Throughout the ages, there have been forecasters willing to exploit our hopes and fears about the future. They have always recognized that it is human nature to dread the unknown. In the 1980s such forecasters recognized that, for most of us, the future was looking less and less certain. We were becoming increasingly anxious about it. These forecasters followed in the old tradition of oracles, magicians, prophets, priests, and assorted others. Using the media to gain access to millions of people, they encouraged a dependence on their "unique" ability to decipher the hidden signs that revealed the future.

Mark Twain once said that laws and sausage were two things he never wanted to see being made. If he were around today, Twain might well extend his statement to include trend forecasting. It is difficult to get futurists to share their forecasting techniques because, for all their seemingly scientific formulas and meticulous calibrations, these techniques are not nearly as scientific and sophisticated as these futurists would have us believe. Some reach their conclusions by clipping and counting news articles. Others conduct interviews, poll experts, or hold focus groups to discover what experts or consumers believe is on the horizon. And some simply identify what will sell with their clients or the public. Because futurists rarely publicize their methodologies, it is difficult for others to test their conclusions.

There is another reason to be careful when approaching megatrends. Many forecasters are unaware of the extent to which their own biases and assumptions color their views of the world and influence their forecasts. For example, just before the Gulf War, I attended a strategic planning retreat for top executives of an international corporation. The company's senior economic consultant presented a classic economic forecast — long, monotonous, statistic-laden, and laced with dozens of unreadable graphs and charts on overhead transparencies.

Even though the future direction of this multibillion dollar company was to be established on the basis of this set of forecasts, no one asked any probing questions. All corporate participants sat passively taking notes. Finally, I dared to ask about the assumptions on which these predictions were based. Annoyed at this challenge to his expertise but nonetheless well prepared, the consultant produced the following overhead transparency:

Long-Term Global Assumptions Upon Which Forecasts Are Based

1. No major armed conflicts.

2. Normal agricultural crop and livestock production worldwide.

3. Real price of crude oil maintained at current level.

4. Foreign exchange value of the U.S. dollar maintained at recent levels.

5. Growth in value and volume of world trade.

Amazingly, in a room filled with senior executives whose futures depended on this set of assumptions, nobody wanted to discuss them. Not a single person asked, "What do you consider the range of 'normal' agricultural production, and what impact could it have on our plans if production strayed outside that range?" Or "What do you consider a 'major armed conflict,' and how would our business be affected if it were to occur?" Or "What would happen to our strategic plan if we base it on the price of crude oil remaining constant and it does not?"

Why did these executives not challenge the forecaster's assumptions? One answer is that they were in a traditionally structured organization where experts were revered. An authority's expertise was, by definition, indisputable. Also they did not challenge his assumptions because they were more comfortable addressing a limited number of clearly enumerated probabilities than exploring a wider range of possible, probable, and preferable futures. Another reason is that they valued products over process: as long as the expert produced charts and graphs, they were satisfied. They risked their own professional futures and their organization's viability by failing to examine the assumptions of the forecaster.

Subsequent global events rendered this forecaster's assumptions useless, illustrating how the belief in trends as "the future" — and in the power of experts who can reveal them to us — can be dangerous. But my deepest concern about the last decade's preoccupation with megatrends is the devastating way it has eroded our sense of efficacy. By encouraging us to believe that the future is shaped primarily by forces outside of our control, the megatrends message has led us to conclude that there is little we can do to shape our future.

The negative impact of this message was magnified by the fact that the megatrends peddlers emerged at a point in history when many of us were already feeling out of control in our lives. An increasing number of us felt that big business was controlling the economy. We felt that national and international leaders manipulated the workings of government. We believed that technology was increasingly depersonalizing our lives. The rate of change was accelerating at a speed that made our heads spin and made us feel that we could not keep up with anything anymore. No wonder, then, that we also accepted the megatrends message that large-scale trends — also beyond our influence — controlled the future.

This kind of thinking has had an enormously harmful effect on civic participation and people's sense of their ability to effect change. In the 1980s, polls showed that the majority of young Americans thought they could have little impact on the future. Record numbers of adults, believing that their input did not really matter, failed to vote. Sociologists have even suggested that the personal greed and "me-ism" that characterized the decade resulted from the generalized feeling that individuals' actions mattered little in the larger scheme of things.

As we face new dilemmas in our business and personal lives, we continue to turn to futurists to provide answers, formulas, and guidance. Initially, we may feel soothed by the part of the megatrend message that assures us that someone out there knows what is going to happen in the future. But ultimately, the part of the message that we are not among those who can comprehend or shape the future increases our feelings of frustration, dissatisfaction, and powerlessness. Focusing predominantly on trends leaves little room for human choice or chance as codeterminants of the future. The megatrend view of the future places us in a reactive mode rather than a proactive one. It increases our sense of dependence on the forecasters instead of leading us to develop the skills and gain the perspectives we need to make wiser choices.

Although consultants and futurists continue to churn out their predictions, more and more people are beginning to realize that trends need to be placed in the context of other forces forging the future. We are beginning to understand the proper and more limited role of trends — as a source of information we can use to make wiser choices. More and more of us are learning to accept responsibility for managing change. We are recognizing that we will have to learn to live with ambiguity and uncertainty and that no expert can give us simple answers about what the future holds.

Individuals and organizations that view trends as only one way of looking at alternative futures empower themselves to take a more active role in determining their future. By placing probabilities in the context of possibilities and preferabilities, we break the spell that the megatrend view has held over us for more than a decade. And we develop a more realistic view of how change *really* takes place, emphasizing the tremendous opportunities and responsibilities each of us has in building the future.

Today, people everywhere are ready for this new message. We are eager for a better future and are willing to play a part in rebuilding our lives, our communities, our nation, and the world. We are ready to break out of the megatrends mold.

CHAPTER FOUR

Preferabilities: Guiding Visions

The future has always been shaped by those who were driven by their visions. Artists, scientists, authors, architects, and filmmakers have shared their visions for the future through the works they produced. Political and social leaders have communicated them through words and actions.

President John F. Kennedy, for example, expressed a clear vision for the future when he said in 1961, "I believe that this nation should commit itself to achieve a goal, before this decade is out, of landing a man on the moon and returning him safely to Earth." His brief statement was a complete vision in that it included *who* (this nation), *what* (land a man on this moon), *when* (by the end of the decade), and *by what standard* (return him safely). Likewise, Dr. Martin Luther King, Jr.'s "I Have A Dream" speech communicated a powerful vision of what one man wanted for his people and his nation.

Visions must inspire and motivate action. They must come as much from the heart as from the head. They can be intellectually analyzed and objectively critiqued, but to be powerful they must be *felt*. The more positive, complete, and compelling a vision is, the more people will be driven to achieve it. Visions are not merely business objectives; they must transcend the bottom line. Daniel Burnham, responsible for planning an exposition for the last turn of the century, said, "Make no small plans. They do not have the magic to stir men's souls."

While visions have always been important, they are more essential today than ever. As the rate of change in the world accelerates and the future seems increasingly uncertain, it becomes more important to have a clear sense of where we want to go. Perhaps in a slower, more predictable world, people could afford to drift and see where the winds might take them. Today, however, positive visions of what we want for the future hold the key to keeping our attention and actions focused.

Our visions should guide us in everything we do, whether it is raising children, managing employees, developing a new product, or participating in civic and religious activities. Without long-term goals that keep us on track, we risk falling farther and farther behind, reacting to an ever-growing list of short-term demands. In a world where unlimited products, problems, and passions compete for our attention, every action we take should be guided by our image of what we want in the future.

Regardless of what we may conclude from the megatrends message, visions, or what I refer to here as "preferabilities," are extremely valuable. A simple illustration is the story of a young man named Rick, who was a student in a futures-global education curriculum I directed. At the age of 13, Rick decided that he wanted to become a professional basketball player, although he was all of 5 feet 6 inches tall and showed little potential for growing tall enough to compete.

In a meeting with Rick and his parents, who discouraged his dreams about basketball, I introduced them to the concept of probabilities and preferabilities. I suggested that trends might suggest that it was unlikely that Rick would ever become a basketball star but that visions led people to accomplish seemingly impossible feats. I suggested that Rick and his parents address both his probable career track and his preferable vision for the future. They did this by agreeing that, if Rick prepared for a more likely career, he could also pursue his basketball ambitions.

Through incessant practice and sheer determination, Rick made the ninth grade team and quickly became its star. At a modest 5 feet 10 inches, Rick made All-State his senior year and received a full basketball scholarship to a prestigious university. Although Rick never made it to the NBA, he did earn an MBA and continues today to take great pleasure in playing basketball.

Rick's story is a good reminder of how acting on our dreams can make them a reality against all odds. Rick is much happier today because he followed his personal dream — however unachievable it might have appeared to others.

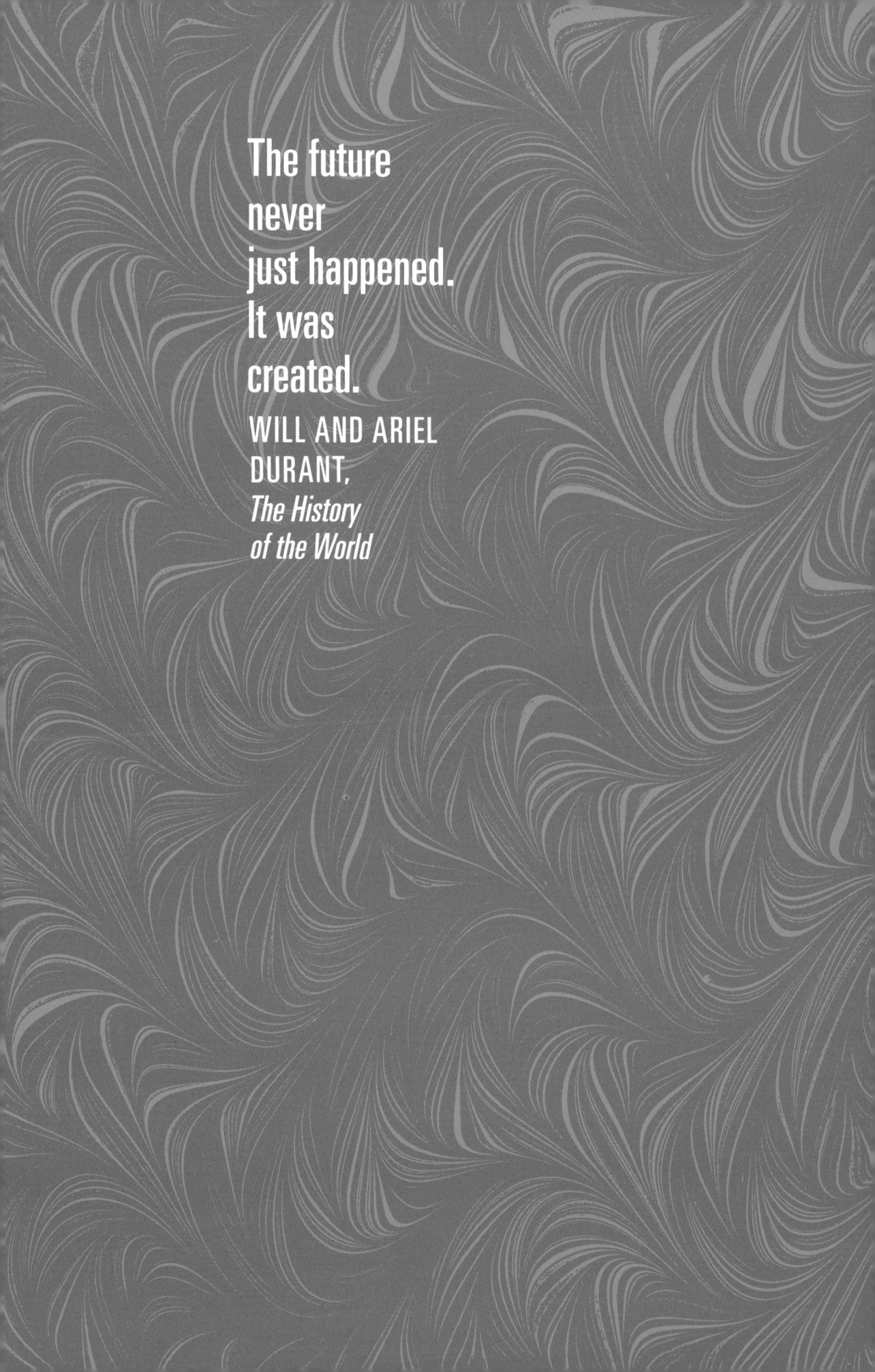

The future
never
just happened.
It was
created.
**WILL AND ARIEL
DURANT,**
*The History
of the World*

As the 1980s unfolded, the signs that the United States was suffering from a lack of shared vision became evident. Leaders in government, business, religion, arts, and education were not engaged in defining and achieving positive, common goals. Tragically, leaders at the highest levels trivialized goal-setting by sarcastically referring to "the vision thing." They suggested that creating visions for the future was New Age hocus-pocus, certainly not something "normal" people did. As a result, the vision void was filled by those who held negative, self-serving goals for the future. We witnessed scandals in sports, business, religion, banking, government, philanthropy — in virtually every area of society where those who had their own interests in mind could step in and fill the gap created by a lack of shared vision and accountability.

Not having a clearly articulated vision for our nation led to tremendous demoralization. The presidential election in the fall of 1992 finally focused attention on the nation's lack of a collective vision. The American people demonstrated that they were hungry for a fresh vision that meshed with their view of the world, that lifted them up from the problems and divisions of the past, and offered them an opportunity to work together to build a better future.

There is growing evidence of a new commitment to building and communicating a common vision. Citizens are speaking out on what they believe; they are recognizing that too many of those in power have clung to old patterns of top-down leadership. Voters are bombarding the White House and Congress with their opinions on every conceivable issue. At all levels, people want to be engaged in defining and realizing preferabilities for the future.

A good example of this shift in attitude is the citizen involvement exhibited recently in a large Midwestern city. Undertaking a large-scale planning process, municipal officials hired a consulting firm to examine trends in building development, road construction, population, schools, and city services and then project them 10 years into the future.

The portrait that the consultants painted of the community's future was based on the simple extrapolation of current trends into the future — probabilities. This emphasis on probabilities triggered a tremendous outcry among the citizens who lived in the community. They challenged the consultants' assumption that the future of their city could be determined merely by projecting patterns of the past into the future. The citizens charged that the consultants had ignored their *preferabilities.* They organized public forums for community members to discuss questions such as, What do we want our community to be like in the future? Can we influence its future if we do not like where the trends might be taking us? Is our path already set, as our planners have assumed? These questions struck such a chord among the general public that municipal leaders scurried to incorporate "public vision sessions" into their strategic planning process.

If community members had not been outspoken about their desire to explore possibilities and preferabilities, the planners would have produced an expensive report that was more a description of past trends than a prescription for future directions. It would have become quickly outdated and would have neither energized nor unified the community. Today, the potential for positive change in that city is much greater as a result of citizen involvement and insistence on developing a guiding vision.

Fortunately, more and more of us are recognizing the need to explore possibilities and preferabilities along with probabilities. Like good athletic coaches, leaders in all fields are beginning to appreciate that visualizing the future is the key to improving performance.

Not long ago, it was common for coaches to berate athletes in front of their teammates. The poor athlete who had been singled out would be mortified, while his teammates watched in horror. There is more and more evidence that focusing on faulty performances does not improve anyone's skill and damages morale and team unity. Effective coaches today believe that athletic success hinges on vision — that being able to imagine oneself performing well is the key to better performance. Many coaches contend that, for top athletes, more than 90 percent of the game is mental. Olympic coaches report that the margin of victory is in the athlete's ability to visualize — to focus her or his mind on what a perfect performance looks and feels like. To nurture this discipline, coaches encourage athletes to practice mental imagery, picturing themselves performing at peak levels.

Each of us needs to practice this same skill, mentally stretching to imagine ourselves at our best. Developing this ability is one of the greatest challenges facing both individuals and organizations. As the world becomes increasingly uncertain, the rate of change accelerates, and the competing demands on our time and attention multiply, preferabilities become ever more important. Our visions become the standard we can use to measure every choice we make and every action we take.

CHAPTER FIVE

Four Futures Formulas

From the clothes we wear to the cars we drive, from how we vote to our interpersonal relationships — nearly every aspect of our lives is shaped by how we view the future. Our unconscious assumptions about what the future holds and how it is formed determine our personal, professional, and civic actions.

I was recently reminded how our images of the future shape our behavior in the present — and can actually determine our future. Mark, a friend of mine who lives near Central Park in New York City, is an avid jogger who runs in the park every morning. Over the last several years, he has become increasingly anxious about being mugged while jogging. As a precaution, he began wearing a jogging suit that had a Velcro-fastened shoulder pocket for his wallet and keys. One misty morning Mark was jolted out of his runner's trance by a stranger who emerged from the fog and collided with him head-on, knocking him down. As Mark picked himself up, he noticed that his pocket was gaping. Although his keys were at the bottom, his wallet was nowhere to be found. Infuriated, he turned and pursued his attacker. When Mark caught the man, who was wide-eyed in terror, he grabbed him angrily, swore at him, and demanded the wallet — which the man quickly produced. Mark wrested the wallet from the stranger's grip, shoving him away in disgust. Then Mark raced home, his heart pounding furiously.

Mark's entire trip home was filled with thoughts about how he *knew* this would happen some day. Only when he stormed into his bedroom and saw his own wallet sitting on his dresser did he realize what he had perpetrated. He had so feared a mugging that he had actually manufactured one. Opening the wallet, the first thing he saw was a photo of his victim's wife and four children, sweetly smiling out at him.

Like Mark, we all carry around images of the future that shape our current realities. If we expect negative things to occur, they usually do. If we look for opportunities and positive experiences, we usually find them. Our actions are influenced by our beliefs about how the future is determined. In fact, our views of what decides the future place most of us into one of four distinct camps.

Roller Coaster Riders

Roller Coaster Riders believe that the future is predetermined by forces beyond our control. The megatrend view of the future has swelled their ranks. For this group, how the future is formed can be reduced to the simple equation:

Future = Trends

Members of this camp imagine time to be like a roller coaster. The tracks have already been laid. All that remains is for people to hang on during the ride, as the present plunges into the future. Roller Coaster Riders believe they have no influence over the direction or speed of their trip. They believe that the only thing they may be able to control is their safety during the journey, so they make sure that their seat belts are firmly fastened. Some members of this group may try to predict where the tracks will take them next. Others simply comment on the quality of their ride, sometimes screaming (with delight or fear) as they race over the tracks.

Some Roller Coaster Riders believe that the course of the future is preset by forces other than trends. One subgroup of riders, for instance, believes that the future has been ordained by God. I recall my puzzlement at this attitude as shared by an entire culture. I was helping the government of a Buddhist nation develop safety and health standards for the construction industry and was visiting construction sites around the country. As I interviewed injured workers or the surviving family members of workers who had been killed in construction accidents, I began to learn what the roller coaster view

SECTION 2

The Nature of Contemporary Change

grant, you could not lose. Only the Navigators in the crowd asserted that they would work their hardest to obtain a grant while acknowledging that other forces could affect the results.

Today's world calls for the Navigator's approach to the future. The ability to seize opportunities presented by rapidly changing and often unexpected events is vital. More and more of us need to become Navigators and believe that the future lies in our own hands.

Navigators understand that the major forces shaping the future are not large-scale trends or the headline-grabbing deeds of world leaders. They recognize that the future is determined day by day, inch by inch, goal by goal, through the incremental choices made by ordinary people.

Olaf Helmer, German-born cofounder of the Institute for the Future and America's first professor of futures research, summarized the need for the Navigator's view when he said, "There is a whole spectrum of possible futures, with varying degrees of probability [and] through proper planning we may exert considerable influence over these possibilities . . . . We must cease to be mere spectators in our own ongoing history and participate with determination in molding the future."

they understand that they can never fully control all of the things that may happen to them, they *choose* to be lucky by deciding to be in the right place at the right time. They intentionally try to "attract" good fortune, often by searching for opportunities in situations where others see only problems. They act while others dawdle or complain.

Navigators believe that unintentional as well as intentional choices shape the future. For example, they understand that people who are indifferent to the effect of their actions on the environment are shaping the future as much as those who are concerned. Individuals who carelessly litter, waste energy, and discard recyclable materials have as powerful an impact on the future as do those who are environmentally conscious.

In fact, Navigators understand that it is nearly impossible *not* to affect the future. From their perspective, not choosing is a choice. And the choice of not choosing has consequences, just as other choices do. For example, not exercising the right to vote still affects the outcome of an election. Not choosing to leave a bad relationship or job is, in effect, a choice to remain in it. Organizations that do not choose to change unproductive patterns or remove ineffective leaders are likewise deciding. Nations that do not choose to deal with tough economic, political, or social issues similarly are charting a course for their future just as surely as if they had selected a more proactive approach.

When we adopt the Navigator's view of the future, we begin to understand that most of the choices we make about ourselves, our organizations, our nations, and the world are not one-time decisions. Just as if we were steering a ship, we must continuously recheck our position, reconfirm our destination, and readjust our course. Almost every goal we hope to achieve will be reached gradually, through decisions we make every day. Whether we want to earn an advanced degree, lower last year's golf handicap, write a book, reduce crime in our neighborhoods, or save the world's rain forests, we accomplish our goals incrementally.

These four views of the future can be seen in our day-to-day actions at work and play. At a professional conference I recently addressed, I witnessed the unexpected announcement of a grant program for participants. The range of responses was remarkable. A few industry leaders seated in front of me, probably Roller Coaster Riders, immediately concluded that the grant recipients must have already been determined, making their own applications for a grant a useless exercise. Others nearby, obviously Crap Shooters, also expressed a lack of interest, declaring that applying was too much a shot in the dark. The voices of a few Masters of the Universe could be heard in the crowd, asserting that if you set your mind to getting a

They hold a fourth view of the future. Navigators try to make informed choices about what they want for the future, taking into account trends and chance. A formula for the navigator's view of the future is:

> **Future = Trends + Chance + Choice**

Navigators decide where they want to go, determine where they are, and then chart a course to their destination. They assess their skills and experience. They collect data that may be helpful on their journey. Navigators recognize and welcome the fact that there will be many choices to make during their journey. They decide the route they want to take, the kind of transportation they will need, and the crew and supplies they may require.

By understanding that the future is shaped by the integration of trends, chance, and choice, Navigators grasp the extraordinary importance of human choice. They believe that making intentional choices prevents them from allowing trends and luck to be the sole determinants of their future.

For example, if one has a history of adult diabetes and believes that nothing can be done to influence the chance of getting the disease, the matter is relegated entirely to chance and trends (genetics). From the Navigator's perspective, this is an abdication of personal responsibility. A Navigator would strive to reduce the likelihood of getting diabetes by taking specific steps in pursuit of good health, such as modifying diet, exercising regularly, and having frequent checkups. Navigators understand that such activities cannot guarantee that they will not get diabetes, because they also acknowledge the role of trends and chance in shaping the future. But they enjoy the peace of mind that comes from knowing that they have taken every conceivable step to create the outcomes they desire.

Navigators take a proactive stance toward the future, approaching their destination by maximizing the impact of their choices. They believe that trends, though not the primary determinant of the future, can provide useful information to help them make better decisions for the future. Navigators do not merely react to trends, they examine them for any opportunities or dangers they may present and then act decisively to exploit those opportunities or neutralize those dangers.

Because they recognize that chance is one of the factors shaping the future, Navigators accept — indeed, they expect — the unexpected. Just as they use trends to make better decisions, they also make choices about chance. Even though

These people might be called Masters of the Universe, after Sherman McCoy, the central character in Tom Wolfe's book, *The Bonfire of the Vanities,* who imagines that he can be and do anything. Filled with arrogance, McCoy begins to consider himself above mere mortals. He is convinced that anything he wants he can have and that anything that happens to him is a direct result of his wishes.

Masters of the Universe, like Wolfe's character, believe they have chosen everything that happens to them, either good or bad. When things are going well, the Masters-of-the-Universe approach to the future serves to boost self-confidence, but it also promotes self-delusion. Television advertisements are filled with promoters hawking "you-can-be-anything-you-want-to-be" books, tapes, and other products that promise to make us wealthy and happy by changing our attitudes.

This approach has adverse consequences. Because it holds us personally responsible for 100 percent of what happens to us, it blames us when we experience accidents, catastrophic illnesses, and other negative events. Masters of the Universe do not believe in happenstance. If something bad occurs, it is because we had negative thoughts or wanted to fail. Masters of the Universe can never say to themselves, "Well, I did the best I could, but it still did not work out," because they believe that we invite into our lives everything that happens, both positive and negative.

For example, a woman I know had been thoroughly indoctrinated into the Masters-of-the-Universe view through a New Age self-empowerment philosophy. When she discovered that she had cancer, her gurus insisted that it was because she had unconsciously wished to be ill. They told her she was fully responsible for healing herself by reprogramming her mind. Her depression deepened as she unsuccessfully tried to rid herself of the disease by "willing" it away. Instead of feeling a greater sense of control over her life, she was racked with guilt for being unable to eradicate something she was taught she had brought upon herself.

Navigators

Roller Coaster Riders, Crap Shooters, and Masters of the Universe are like the blind men in the Indian folk tale, each of whom uses his hands to examine a different part of an elephant. The blind men describe very different creatures to one another. Each is correct in his description as far as it goes, but none has the whole truth. The truth about the future is that it is determined by the interplay of trends, chance, and choice.

People who recognize this can be called Navigators.

looked like when taken to a societal level. Everyone seemed to accept the injuries and deaths as preordained experiences the accident victims needed in this lifetime in order to evolve to higher levels in future lifetimes — and therefore nobody was held responsible for the accidents!

Crap Shooters

A second group of people, the Crap Shooters, share a very different view of how the future is formed. They do not believe it is predetermined, waiting to be revealed to us. On the contrary, they see the future as random, like throwing dice in a game of craps. From their point of view, there is neither rhyme nor reason to what occurs in life. Crap Shooters recognize only chance as the determinant of future events. The formula for describing their view of the future is:

> **Future = Chance**

Crap Shooters believe that it is futile for us to plan our vacations, our businesses, or our lives. To them, striving for control in a chaotic world is engaging in self-delusion.

Crap Shooters can sometimes sound and act like Roller Coaster Riders, because individuals in both groups share the belief that the future is not influenced significantly by human choice. For instance, people who ask, "Why should I quit smoking? When my time is up, it's up," could be Roller Coaster Riders, believing that *someone* has predetermined their precise moment and mode of death, or they could be Crap Shooters, believing the future to be random and senseless. An observer would have to probe their thoughts further to be able to ascertain which of the two views they held. One thing is certain: individuals in both groups acknowledge little, if any, human role in shaping the future and do not readily accept responsibility for their own actions.

Masters of the Universe

A third group of people share yet another view of the future. These people do not accept either trends or chance as the predominant influences on the future. They recognize only human choice. A formula for their view is:

> **Future = Choice**

MYTH #2: We Cannot Understand the Nature of Contemporary Change.

Many prognosticators, futurists, forecasters, and megatrend wizards would have us believe that only they understand the nature of change and its implications for the future. This second megatrends myth, that ordinary people cannot comprehend the nature of contemporary change, is dangerous and erroneous. Although it may serve the interests of the experts, it does not serve the rest of us, nor does it benefit society at large. Its major consequence is that we defer to others to analyze and solve our personal, professional, and civic dilemmas rather than building our own skills and trusting our own perceptions.

There is no evidence that experts, regardless of their credentials or intelligence, know what the future holds any more than the rest of us. More than at any time in history, the patterns and trends of the past cannot be counted on to continue into the future. Experts on *what was* are no more likely to know *what will be* than the rest of us. Every day, political, economic, technological, medical, and sociological events and discoveries are surprising even the more reknown experts in those fields.

How, then, can any sense be made of this time in which we live? If the future is so uncertain, how can we plan at all? Do the changes we are experiencing share any characteristics that can help us comprehend them?

This section of the book explores the nature of change

in today's world. It examines the ideas and images that guided our behavior in the past — and those that seem to be shaping our behavior today — and looks at their implications for contemporary life. It examines the basic paradigm that undergirds our society and proposes a new paradigm for the 21st century, one that is more consistent with the way that people and organizations actually operate.

CHAPTER SIX

The Characteristics of Contemporary Change

One of my clients recently declared in frustration, "I want to change in order to meet the future, but the future keeps getting here before I'm ready for it!" Is the rate of change actually accelerating? Have all generations felt this way, or is there something unique about ours?

There are five significant characteristics of contemporary change. The first and foremost is the rate at which change is occurring. If there were a single word to describe life today, it would be *changing*. It has almost become a cliché to say that the rate of change is accelerating at breakneck speed. We are flooded by more information than we can process. There are too many decisions to be made, too many demands on our time. We cannot keep up with anything — from birthdays to paying the bills. We feel squeezed by having more and more to do in less and less time. We cannot seem to stay current in our careers, no matter how many professional journals we read or conferences we attend. Organizations are being restructured so frequently that we cannot recall which ones are still in business. We cannot remember which nations have ceased to exist, and we can no longer turn to our atlas because it may be obsolete by the time of printing. The most unquestionable certainties of the past seem to be eroding.

To illustrate how rapidly change is occurring, it is useful to take an historical perspective. Imagine the entire existence of Earth as occurring in a single year. Midnight January 1 would represent the origin of the planet, and midnight December 31 would represent the present. Each day in that single year would then equal 12 million years of actual history. Earliest life forms, simple bacteria, would first appear in February, and fish, a more complex life form, would not appear until November 20. Dinosaurs would arrive on December 10 and become extinct by Christmas Day. Our first recognizable ancestors would not appear until the evening of December 31 — the last day of the year — and Homo sapiens would not show up until 11:45 p.m. *All recorded history would occur after 11:59 p.m., in the final minute of the year!* Within a millisecond of the last minute of this condensed year — our lifetime — comes the introduction of global transportation, electronic communications, weapons of mass destruction, space travel, and vast numbers of medical and biomedical breakthroughs.

Computers and satellites have enabled more people than ever before to disseminate and receive information, spreading it instantaneously — and to the most remote parts of the world. These changes have been so pervasive and life-altering that we forget how recent a phenomenon they are — not only in the history of the planet, but even in our own lifetimes. We forget that many people are alive today who witnessed the introduction of airplanes, televisions, and computers.

So accustomed have we become to our plugged-in, fast-paced life that it seems inconceivable that we never came in contact with computers until relatively recently. It seems like lifetimes ago that I wrote everything out on a yellow pad, which then had to be retyped, draft after draft, on a typewriter. Yet the IBM personal computer was introduced as recently as 1981. Only two years before that, I struggled to get the large university where I was completing my dissertation to adjust their rules so that I could submit the first dissertation printed on a computer. Today, nobody would dream of tackling such a project manually!

The second characteristic of change today is that change itself is undergoing a transformation. We are not only experiencing the same kinds of changes at a faster rate; we are experiencing changes that are *qualitatively* different from anything previous generations knew. We are moving from industrial-based national economies to a single, information-based global economy. This shift is causing unprecedented changes in every arena. We cannot forecast what the future holds for us politically, economically, socially, or technologically based on the past because the era we are moving into is strikingly different from any we have known.

Furthermore, an increasing number of globally significant changes today are the result of human actions, whereas changes of the past were caused primarily by natural phenomena. Thinking back to the condensed, one-year history of planet Earth, we can see that only in our own lifetime — the last fraction of the last second of the last minute of the year — has humanity moved from living in a natural environment to a manufactured one. We are the first generation in history whose major challenges are a direct consequence of our own technology, lifestyles, and actions. Even the most remote parts of the world have not escaped the consequences of modern technology, including pollution.

In their book *New Mind, New World,* Paul Ehrlich and Robert Ornstein argue that humankind has reached a point where it has outstripped its ability to understand or control the world it has created. Humankind evolved as the fittest survived. Over millennia, those who passed their genes on to future generations were those best able to solve the kinds of natural problems that our predecessors faced — a bear at the entrance to the cave, a flood on the river banks, a fire sweeping the plains. Over time, the human brain developed the skill to cope with just those kinds of problems: immediate, visible dangers that could be resolved through quick action.

Today these kinds of problems no longer pose the greatest threat to our existence. Our world, more than that of any previous generation, is manufactured — a world of our own creation. And it is increasingly difficult to manage. Now the greatest dangers facing humanity are immense, invisible, diffuse, interconnected, long term, and *created by humans.* However difficult it is to respond to floods or hurricanes, it is extraordinarily more complicated to address meltdowns at nuclear power plants, ethnic cleansing in foreign lands, and unemployment, hunger, and homelessness in our own cities. Our minds cannot easily grasp nor readily solve such problems. We have built a world we have trouble comprehending, let alone controlling.

Our utmost commitment and skill are required to understand today's challenges. Our very survival depends on our ability to adapt our minds, which are successful at solving simple problems, to address the complex, interrelated issues of today.

The third characteristic of contemporary change is the increasing interconnectedness of issues, events, and cultures. Nations and national economies do not — and cannot — exist in isolation. The New York-London stock market no longer dominates international finance. Increasingly, Japan and other Asian countries sit at the economic table as full partners, holding a significant number of chips (computer and otherwise).

Europe is on its way to becoming an economic United States of Europe, with common currencies, common trading agendas, and coordinated economies. Scientific and environmental issues are increasingly — and necessarily — multinational in scope. Industrial cartels and conglomerates can no longer survive by producing goods in only one country.

Consider, for example, how difficult it is to identify exactly how "American" an automobile is today. U.S. manufacturers produce cars overseas for both foreign and domestic markets. They also assemble cars in the United States from parts made in other countries. And foreign auto manufacturers import cars to the United States that contain parts manufactured in the United States. Foreign auto companies assemble cars in the United States, using parts made here, abroad, or both. To add to the confusion, many American and foreign manufacturers have forged such complicated alliances that they are often competitors and collaborators simultaneously. The "Buy American" slogan really means, "Buy American — sort of."

This interdependence can be seen in virtually every arena. Public education, for example, cannot improve without the serious commitment of government, business, and community. To improve education, we must reach beyond traditional curricular issues into such areas as cultural diversity, changing student populations, nutrition, child care, crime, child abuse, race, ethnicity, physical and emotional disabilities, classroom technology, teacher education and certification, educators' unions, funding, regulatory statutes, AIDS, sex education, prenatal care, and employment — to name just a few.

The same complexity and interconnectedness characterize such issues as economic growth, environmental quality, health care, public safety — virtually every aspect of our lives. Touching one part of society affects all other parts. We can no longer afford to tackle any issue in isolation.

Even on a personal level, individuals are discovering how each part of their lives is inextricably intertwined with every other part. Health issues affect us at work, and our attitudes and behaviors at work affect our health. Our financial security is often related to personal and professional risk-taking. Our personal happiness is tied to feeling valued in the workplace. Each aspect of our lives is linked to every other, shaped by previous choices, and entangled in a web extending from the past into the future.

The fourth characteristic of change today is that its complexity often causes things to be other than what they appear to be. In a world changing as rapidly as ours, reliance on traditional assumptions and generalizations can get us into trouble.

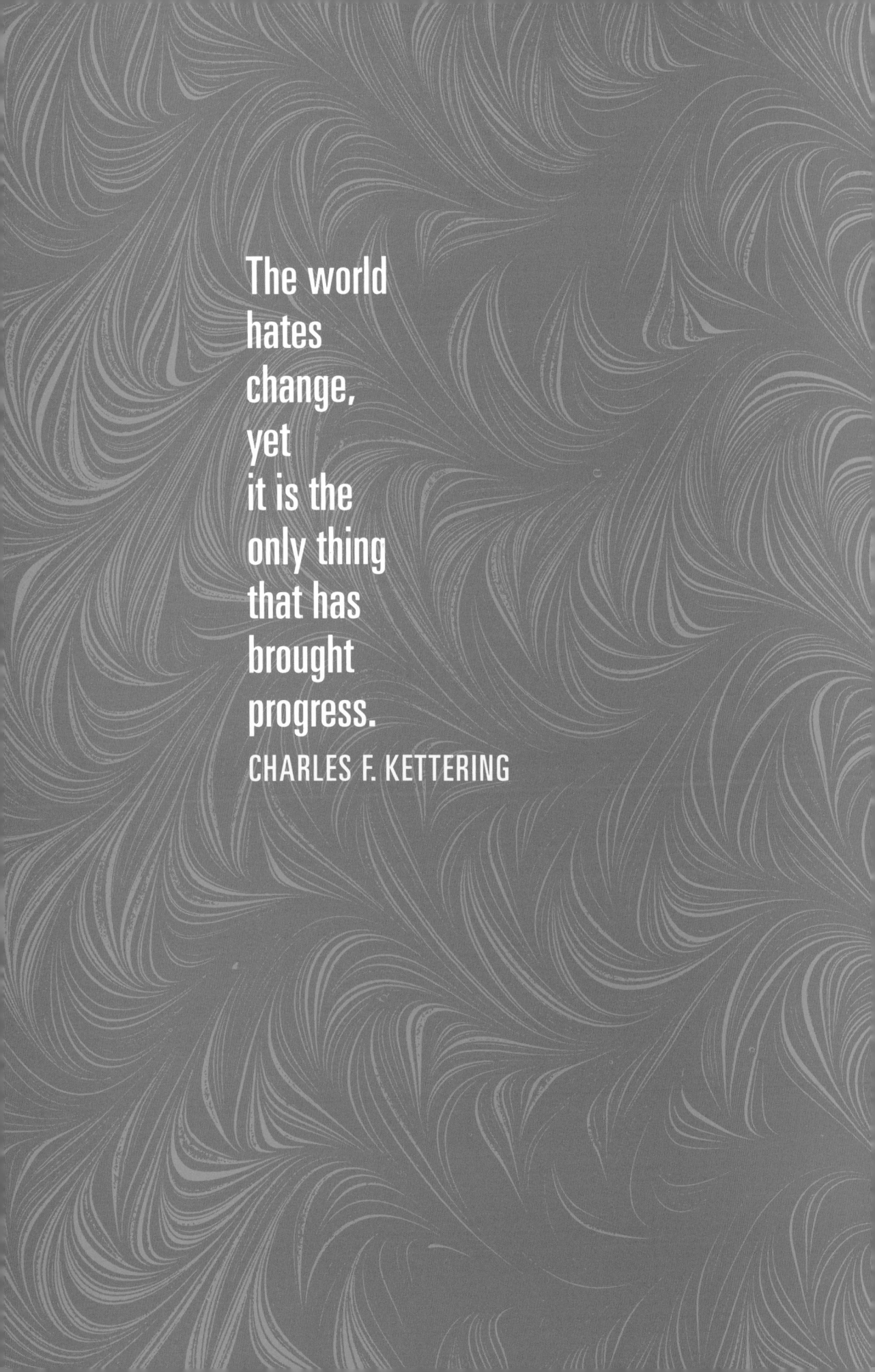

The world
hates
change,
yet
it is the
only thing
that has
brought
progress.
CHARLES F. KETTERING

One illustration of how misleading casual assumptions can be is my experience one fading Sunday afternoon while driving from the Eastern Shore of Maryland back to Washington, D.C. Pulling a trailer twice the size of my car, I was moving slowly in the right-hand lane of a four-lane highway. Traffic was routinely speeding past me in the left lane until a car pulled up alongside mine and maintained the same pace I was traveling, thus forming a moving blockade, preventing all other cars from passing. Soon a long line of hostile motorists formed behind us. As the procession continued, drivers began shouting, honking, flashing headlights, and waving fists in the air. The driver of the car next to me remained undaunted, ignoring their protests and continuing to prevent them from passing us.

After a sharp bend in the road, we all discovered what his radar detector or CB radio must have warned him about: at least 10 troopers were pulling speeding motorists over left and right. The shoulder of the road looked like a parking lot. After we had passed the commotion, my blockade partner pulled in front of me, releasing a floodgate of suddenly grateful motorists. As each car went by, people who had only moments before been cursing the dilatory driver now treated him like a hero, waving and shouting thanks.

Just as this driver was not what he appeared to be, many situations we encounter are other than what they seem on the surface. I was reminded again of this lesson while hiking in the Appalachian mountains. I encountered an Asian family along a narrow, wooded path. In a language totally unfamiliar to me, the father and mother were apparently explaining the flora and fauna to their three little children. I smiled at them, and they smiled back. I nodded, and they nodded back. I bowed slightly, and they bowed slightly back. Then, in slow, clearly enunciated English, I asked, "Where...are...you...from?" All four of them responded simultaneously with a perfect Southern drawl, "Charleston."

Because things are increasingly not what they appear to be, a fifth characteristic of contemporary change is that problems often call for counterintuitive solutions. The logical solutions — or those that would have worked in the past — often exacerbate rather than alleviate problems. For example, a local Little League baseball organization decided to tackle a recurring problem head on: coaches had been playing the weaker, less talented kids only in games in which their team was assured victory. Parents, most of whom had children sitting on the bench game after game, worked hard to get the rules changed so that every member of each team would get to play at least part of every game. They reasoned that this approach would provide poorer players a greater opportunity to play, thereby improving their skills and making them feel a more integral part of the team. However, in response to these efforts, within a few weeks most of the coaches had driven the weaker players off their teams through neglect, harassment, or manipulation. Consequently, the strategy backfired. Rather than having the opportunity to play occasionally and feel part of a team, the weaker players ended up unable to play at all. The action taken by the parents, however logical it seemed at the time, ended up hurting the very people it was designed to help because the parents had not understood that they could not change the coaches' overriding drive to win.

Another instance of solutions going against common sense occurred when the public libraries in a Midwestern state began suffering severe financial difficulties due to the economic recession. To economize, the legislature decided to take an ostensibly sensible step. They amended the law so that citizens in one community could use libraries in neighboring communities, thus allowing greater sharing of resources without unnecessary duplication. However, within a short time the libraries deteriorated noticeably. Citizens in poorer communities felt they no longer needed to support their own local libraries because they could go to better facilities in the wealthier neighboring communities. Residents of the wealthier communities became indignant, contending that they were not funding state-of-the art libraries for the use of "outsiders." Rather than support their libraries, these well-to-do citizens decided to privately purchase whatever books and tapes they might want. Within a remarkably short period of time, a first-rate statewide library system had collapsed — which was the exact opposite result that the legislators had intended!

It is imperative that we understand the characteristics of contemporary change. Our only hope of creating a better future is to learn how to manage change wisely. And the first step is to face change squarely and comprehend its many facets.

CHAPTER SEVEN

The Form-Driven Paradigm of the Past

*I*n the last few years, there has been a lot of talk about paradigms. A paradigm is simply a shared view of how the world operates. Our paradigms color everything we experience, like a filter on the lens through which we see and interpret life. Often we are unaware of our paradigms because they are unconscious and shared throughout a culture.

If appropriate to our environment and the times in which we live, a paradigm can help us understand and manage our world. Conversely, obsolete or dysfunctional paradigms can cripple us. Inappropriate assumptions about how the world works cause us to expect people and organizations to behave in ways they never will. Operating on such false assumptions leads to frustration and failure.

For centuries, people in Western nations have shared a view of how nature, organizations, institutions, and society are structured. This view shaped our expectations, our hopes, and our behaviors. Because it was so widely and strongly held, this belief system became not only a description of the way things actually are, but also a prescription for the way things ought to be.

Let's call this view of the world that has dominated our lives the form-driven paradigm because its most notable characteristic is the emphasis on form over function. Wherever we look, we can see that we have adopted a shared belief that form should lead function. We have declared some social units families and others not families because of how they look — not because of how they function. Therefore, two parents living with their children in a home have been deemed a family unit, but a homosexual couple living together or grandparents raising their grandchildren have not qualified as a family. Similarly, we have characterized people who attend church or synagogue as spiritual and those who do not attend as nonspiritual. We have judged people not by who they are but by what they do for a living, their racial or ethnic background, where they live, or what they wear. Form has ruled over function.

This societal emphasis on form — or structure — rather than function — or purpose — has been interwoven with the scientific notions of the last few centuries. Following the views of the 17th-century physicist, Sir Isaac Newton, scientists adopted a metaphor of the universe as a huge machine composed of intricately related components. They promoted the notion that the universe is orderly and can be objectively observed and measured.

Through the years, this scientific theory of an orderly, hierarchical universe has been used to explain interpersonal and organizational behavior. People and organizations have been expected to perform like efficient machines in predictable ways. They have been viewed as the sum of their parts, nothing more and nothing less. Both individuals and organizations have been identified by their visible characteristics — their form. Invisible traits were considered to be unimportant or nonexistent.

Although the form-driven paradigm has existed for centuries, it has become the predominant model in the 20th century. As indigenous cultures have been destroyed and mass media has spread American values worldwide, form-driven institutions have come to dominate the 20th-century landscape. Whether governmental, social, economic, educational, or religious, they were identified by their form or shape. This shape

THE PYRAMID:
The Predominant Form-Driven Model of the 20th Century

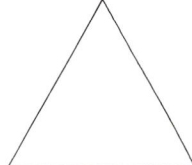

was almost universally pyramidal. The pyramidal model of organization has defined our work, leisure activities, relationships, and concepts of self. It has so permeated our lives that we have come to view it as the natural order of things.

At the dawn of the 20th century, the captains of industry did not confuse form with function. They were clear about their goals and designed structures to achieve them. They knew what they wanted: to retain personal control of their empires while expanding them to unprecedented proportions and capitalizing on new inventions and technologies that greatly increased productivity. They concluded that the perfect organizational structure to accomplish this goal was the pyramidal organization with themselves firmly fixed at the top of the pyramid.

In the early 20th century, Henry Ford applied the pyramidal structure to assembly-line production, making it the dominant model for businesses and institutions. It seemed to be remarkably suited to the manufacture of consumer goods, the primary economic activity during most of the century. Ford's organizational model for the Ford Motor Company was clearly pyramidal, with Ford at the top, alone and in charge. His closest advisors, the company's senior executives, were layered immediately below him. Middle managers came below them. At the very bottom of the pyramid were the greatest number of employees, the assembly-line workers who actually made the automobiles.

A key belief accompanying the form-driven paradigm is that one's position in the structure reflects how intelligent and trustworthy one is. Workers at the bottom of the structure are expected not to think. They are encouraged neither to offer suggestions nor to exercise judgment. Their job is to act as human machines that make a product. As Ford expressed it, "All that we ask of the men is that they do the work which is set before them."

A basic value of the form-driven paradigm is efficiency. Squeezing more out of those at the bottom of the structure results in greater profits for those at the top. The belief has been, *"The more we get out of our workers in the shortest time with the least investment, the greater our profits will be.* Known as a pioneering efficiency expert, Frederick W. Taylor advocated that every job at the bottom of the pyramid should be reduced to its most basic discernible action so that one could determine how quickly each action could be performed. Taylor devised elaborate charts to monitor employees along the assembly line. These were used to ensure that each worker turned the wrench as close to the optimum number of times in an hour as possible. Later in the century, Taylor's theories were applied to mid-level workers through time-management programs. Thus these workers were rewarded only for what could be easily measured.

Taylor's approach was reinforced by the widely accepted notion that science was the key to unlocking the door of progress. Science was viewed as linear, logical, nonintuitive, measurable, and mechanistic. The scientific approach meant breaking everything into its smallest measurable components and managing each of them separately. If something could not be measured, it did not exist or was considered unimportant.

Over time, this preoccupation with efficiency developed into the short-term, quick-profit, bottom-line mentality that has dominated most American corporations until very recently. The business community embraced the notion that profit should be demonstrated on a quarterly basis and valued over other indicators of an organization's health. The goal, which for some corporations nearly became an obsession, was to make substantial profits for the current quarter, even if that short-term profit was earned at the expense of the organization's long-term success. The negative consequences of this approach were rarely considered.

In pyramidal organizations power flows from the top down. Those at the top of the pyramid generally regard the interests of those at the bottom as inconsistent with — indeed, as a threat to — their own. When those at the top invest little in those at the bottom, those at the bottom are forced to operate in isolation with no participation in decision making. Schisms invariably develop in these organizations.

Anyone who enters the pyramid wants to move up as rapidly as possible. Those at the top are hailed as national role models, the embodiment of the American dream. History books are replete with success stories about Vanderbilts, Carnegies, Rockefellers, Mellons, and others who made it to the top of the pyramid during the great Industrial Age.

Yet there is room for only a few at the top. Most of us never make it there, regardless of our ambitions and dreams. Over the years, I have worked with thousands of people who feel trapped at the bottom of the pyramid. They feel powerless, and they do not "own" the organization's products or problems. These workers — *the ones who actually make the product or deliver the service* — are the least valued members of the pyramid. They are paid the least, given the least authority, and incur the greatest health and safety risks.

Conversely, those employees who ascend within the pyramid get farther and farther away from the production process. Their incomes rise, their authority increases, and they are expected to think more and do less manual labor. Thus, in pyramid-shaped structures, "thinkers" are at the top and "doers" are at the bottom. Those at the top are not required to consider if their orders can be carried out; those at the bottom — those who actually know the products or service best — are not expected to solve problems.

Middle managers are trapped between the thinkers above them and the doers below in a kind of organizational no-man's land. As companies grow in size, the pyramid adds layers, further distancing those at the top from those at the bottom. Mid-level managers become bureaucrats who translate the thinkers' goals to the doers, monitor the doers to make sure they do the jobs "right," and then report back to the thinkers on the doers' performance.

Mid-level managers are expected to be ambitious and upwardly mobile. They are encouraged to identify with those above them and remain loyal to lines of command at all costs. As they work their way up the pyramid, they frequently lose touch with those below, who view them with increasing suspicion. In corporations everywhere, mid-level managers struggle with their identity. Many times over the years, I have encountered middle managers who have clung to the point of view of the hourly employees from whose ranks they have risen, only to be warned by their superiors that their future at the company was jeopardized by what the supervisors see as misplaced loyalty.

Senior managers often resent line workers who want to infringe upon management prerogatives, while those on the line resent being patronized and excluded from decision making. Each group distrusts the motives of the other. From these pyramidal relationships ultimately emerged the labor unions and collective bargaining, which have given workers the leverage to improve workplace conditions, safety, wages, and benefits. While traditional labor-management relations have served to bridge the gap between the top and bottom of the pyramid, they certainly have not reduced the adversarial nature of the relationship.

Pyramidal structures also force information to flow in only one direction — from the top down. The thinkers make decisions and communicate them through mid-level management to the doers. Bottom-up information flow is virtually nonexistent, and lateral flow is not much better. This is significant, because poor communication leads to poor cooperation, which very often breeds unhealthy competition between departments within the same institution. In many companies, the "enemy" becomes another branch of the same organization. Three common examples are universities with adversarial departments, auto makers with competing divisions, and the U.S. Armed Forces with legendary rivalry among the branches. This bunker mentality discourages the sharing of ideas and funds. Internal competition for resources, status, and power soon becomes counterproductive.

Because information does not flow upward in pyramidal organizations, corporate executives often hire outside consultants to find out what is going on. In spite of the large sums these consultants are paid, their reports and recommendations are often ignored unless they support what top executives want to hear. The organizational climate in form-driven institutions does not support truth-telling. Employees who report to the top executive often have far too much to lose by telling the truth. Sam Goldwyn once summed up the pyramidal leaders' feelings about honest feedback when he told his staff, "I do not want yes-men around me. I want people who will tell me the truth even if it costs them their job."

In the pyramidal organization, numbers have a magical power. Focus is on those things that can be easily quantified, and data are often collected so as to reinforce current assumptions and beliefs. This was exemplified in the Vietnam War, when the Pentagon insisted on tallying body counts and kill ratios as primary evidence that the United States was winning the war. According to General Norman Schwarzkopf, these official figures were both inflated and misleading.

The tendency to use numbers to support preconceived notions is a characteristic of form-driven organizations. In the early 1970s, it led the American auto industry to interpret its marketing data as showing that American consumers wanted big cars when there was ample evidence to the contrary. Japanese car makers, who conversely did not use figures to bolster their existing beliefs, identified emerging patterns and responded quickly to them. As a result, they made serious inroads in the U.S. auto market.

In form-driven organizations, our value as individuals is defined by our jobs — which also define our places in society. The higher we climb the corporate ladder, the more society values us. As we rise in the corporate world, perquisites like pensions, parking places, company cars, stock options, and keys to the executive washroom grow proportionately. Those deemed valuable enough by the company to hold a washroom key automatically get keys that open the doors to country clubs, service clubs, honorary societies, and political posts and gain a profusion of other social benefits and honors.

The importance of job titles is reflected in many parts of our form-driven society. How many times have you been asked, "What do you do?" when you knew that the questioner really wanted to hear your job title or profession so that he could determine how much status to afford you?

This focus on position in the pyramid is depersonalizing. Recently, while dining with a colleague in the cafeteria of a large federal agency in Washington, D.C., I asked her about a person who looked familiar, seated a few tables away. She was able to pinpoint with great detail the man's position in the organization, his influence, and reputation — but had no idea what his name was!

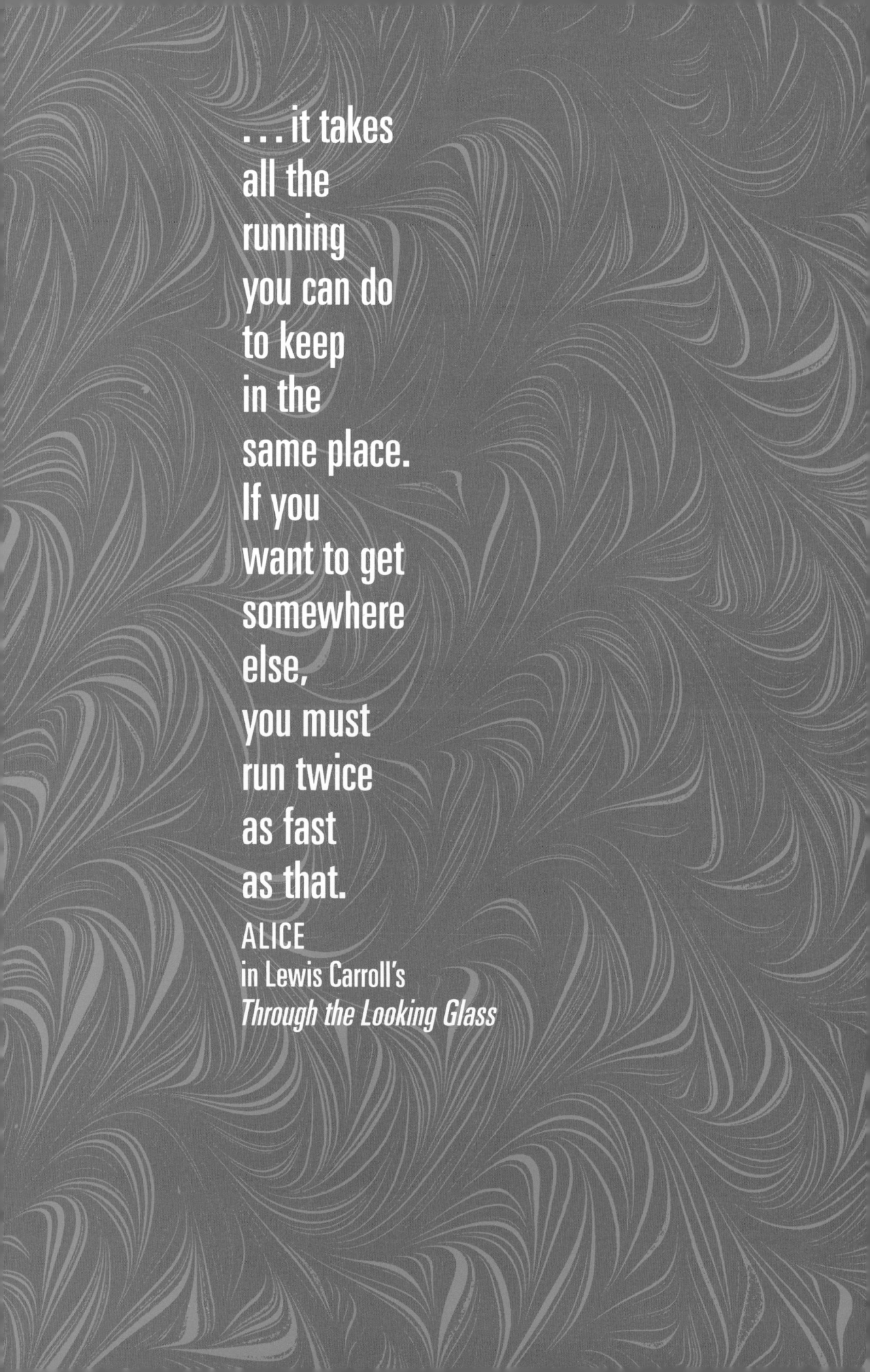

> ...it takes all the running you can do to keep in the same place. If you want to get somewhere else, you must run twice as fast as that.
>
> **ALICE**
> in Lewis Carroll's
> *Through the Looking Glass*

The attention to status generated by pyramidal values has fueled America's growing preoccupation with consumerism. Mass production placed more consumer goods within the reach of a growing middle class. And to keep the capitalist engines purring, higher profits necessitated more products. More products necessitated a focus on consuming. Before long, producing and consuming products became a primary focus of our society. And we have "exported" this value to other countries, looking for wider markets for our products. People all over the world seek readily available, inexpensive manufactured products. Products that had not long before been considered luxuries — or did not even exist — came to be regarded as essentials. People began to think they had a *right* to own a car, a television, or a VCR.

Whatever America's ranking might be in other areas, the United States is still the uncontested front-runner in consumerism. With only 10 percent of the world's population, Americans consume more than 80 percent of its energy. We own one car for every 1.3 people; the average for the rest of the world is one car for every 13 people. We measure our quality of life by the consumer products we own — and we often go into debt in order to own more "things." To satisfy the ever-growing appetite of American consumers over the years, it has become essential to produce more and more products, to build bigger factories, and to keep supply in line with demand, even if quality and safety have to be compromised from time to time.

Our views on consumerism have been radically altered in just a short period of time. Twenty-five years ago a *consumer* was an uncomplimentary term reserved for individuals who were not *producers*. Consumer advocate Ralph Nader was viewed by many with suspicion and as un-American for advocating the belief that American consumers had rights regarding the safety and performance of manufactured products. Many were unsure whom Nader was trying to represent, because few people defined themselves as consumers. Today, Nader's Raiders, his original consumer-protection organization, is called "Public Citizen," using the words *citizen* and *consumer* interchangeably. Rather than being suspect, consumerism has become an integral part of our culture. Hardly a day goes by that the media does not use the term "the American consumer" to mean "citizen." Shopping has become an all-American pastime.

The emphasis on form over function did not occur only in the industrial sector. Government bureaus, school systems, health-care services, justice systems, churches, political parties, and social institutions followed suit. Even many organizations that advocated systemic change themselves adopted pyramidal, paternalistic structures.

Education offers an example of how one institution in our society became increasingly pyramidal. In the 19th century, education in this country was not form-driven. Schools developed as they were needed and functioned independently of one another. Many were one-room schoolhouses where a single teacher taught students of all grades. Teachers answered directly to those who hired them. Lessons in math, science, reading, and other subjects were tied to one another and to practical application beyond the schoolroom walls. The length of the school day and the school year, like the curriculum itself, were determined by societal needs. When youngsters were needed to assist with the crops, the schools closed down.

Over the course of the 20th century, those one-room schoolhouses were closed, smaller districts were consolidated into larger ones, and the ratio of administrators to teachers soared exponentially as the pyramids grew. Superintendents, eager to expand their spheres of influence, annexed neighboring independent schools. Today, the superintendent of schools sits at the top (Henry Ford), with central administrators just below (corporate executives), the building principals below them (middle managers), and the teachers at the bottom (assembly-line workers). Teachers are expected not to question the goals set by those at the top nor to participate in determining the quality, speed, or nature of the instructional process. Teachers are the *doers*. Their task is to perform in individual classrooms the functions that they have been told to perform by those above them. Publishers still brag to administrators that their curriculum materials are "teacher proof." In turn, teachers, in their effort to access power, have formed powerful teachers' unions — themselves mighty pyramid-like fortresses.

As school districts became more pyramidal, teachers were expected to follow the rules, teach by the book, and not make waves. The student, like a car on the assembly line, moved from one classroom to another to be *worked on* through incremental and disconnected applications. What was learned in science, math, social studies, or reading was never related to what was learned in the other classes nor to what was going on in the world outside.

An illustration of the absurdity of this assembly-line approach to education that still haunts me is an incident that occurred one day many years ago. I was visiting the classroom of a fellow teacher when a horrible auto accident took place outside her classroom window. Four cars were entangled with one another — cars that could have been carrying friends or family of the students sitting in that room. Ambulances came and went. The students, some noticeably disturbed, watched the scene in horror while their teacher ignored the drama and continued to follow her manual. When I later asked her about it, she explained that she felt compelled to push forward because she had been required to administer tests the week before and fell behind where the district said she should be in the curriculum.

Competition and distrust among teachers was bred by discouraging them from sharing ideas — or even seeing their fellow teachers teach. Being denied access to office space, phones, technology, and other support caused teachers to feel distrusted and distrustful rather than to develop a sense of professional collegiality. Innovation, creativity, and student performance suffered as a result.

The pyramidal structure caused students to become even more disempowered than their teachers. Predictably, students were inculcated with form-driven values: be on time, follow directions without question, do not take risks, do not question procedures, offer only information that is requested, and mind your own business. Those who challenged these rules were labeled troublemakers and punished, ultimately being forced out of the system if they did not conform.

Other institutions have likewise fallen victim to the form-driven paradigm that dominates our society. Although the captains of industry heralded the pyramidal structure as a means to achieve their desired ends, over the course of the century *the emphasis on form has become an end in and of itself.* We have forgotten that today's organizational structures were designed for specific purposes — purposes that may have ceased to be valid many years ago. Yet we cling to pyramidal structures as if there were no other way to organize. Many people, including world leaders, have come to believe that by building pyramidal organizations they are simply mirroring the natural order of the universe. Alternative structures, like communes or kibbutzim, are often derided for being un-American or unnatural.

Like the Egyptian pyramids, which were constructed by slaves thousands of years ago, the pyramids of this century have become impenetrable, immovable, and long-lasting. Our pyramids were intended to address the needs of an Industrial Age that no longer exists. Pyramidal organizations were built for stable conditions — which rarely exist in today's world. Because the top-down structure isolates those at the top and inhibits free information flow, the typical pyramid organization, when trying to grapple with rapidly changing global issues, is far too slow. It is like a huge animal whose nervous system is so inadequate for its size that it can be half-eaten by a predator before the impulse arrives to its brain that something is wrong.

Those who head pyramidal organizations today arrived there by inching their way to the top; consequently, many of those at the top are committed to this model and believe it brought progress to the world, made America great, and will solve our future problems. The pyramid is all they have ever known. Thus, even when they acknowledge that the pyramid is becoming less effective, these leaders continue to rely on it.

Whether the pyramidal structure was the most effective model for the past is a moot point. We do know that it is increasingly failing to meet the challenges of today and the future. For this reason, some experts are calling for a "flattening out" of organizational charts. They want to change the shape of the pyramid from

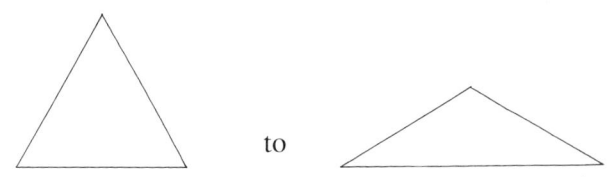

△ to △

These experts can be praised for trying to reduce bureaucracy and inefficiency, or they can be criticized for clinging to the pyramid and catering to those at the top, who remain in control regardless of how many layers are eliminated below them. In reality, the problem is not what shape pyramid an organization is, or even whether it is a pyramid or another form. *The mistake of most of these "experts" is their continued focus on form over function.*

As long as we emphasize structure without first determining the purposes we want our organizations and institutions to serve, restructuring will result in nothing more than rearranging the chairs on the deck of the Titanic.

CHAPTER EIGHT

A Function-Driven Paradigm for the Future

Even when we know intellectually that the world is changing, many of us continue to behave as if we expect the future to be just like the past. Consciously or unconsciously, we hold on to old assumptions, images, and behaviors. However, an increasing number of individuals and organizations are recognizing that the world is not what it has been. They are learning to make the connection between global changes and the new beliefs and behaviors these changes demand of us. They recognize that their old beliefs and assumptions limit their ability to comprehend change and to envision different futures for themselves, their organizations, and their nations.

Form-driven assumptions, values, and behaviors cannot solve the personal, organizational, and global issues we face. We need a new paradigm, a fresh set of shared values and beliefs about how people and organizations behave — a set of beliefs that accurately describes the world and will be useful into the 21st century.

The call for a new set of beliefs has been called a "paradigm shift" by authors, philosophers, and social commentators who are clear about its need but less clear about what it is and how it occurs. More and more of them are eager to reject the pyramid as a prescription for organizational effectiveness. They are equally enthusiastic about replacing it with their own alternative models with names like "cellular organizations," "the matrix model," and "molecular management." They want to replace

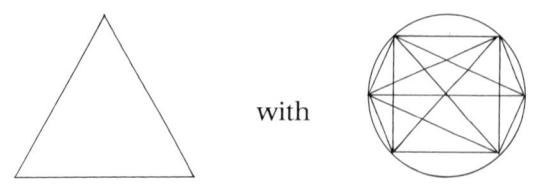

△ with ⊕

or some variation thereof.

These thinkers are correct to suggest that we reject the pyramid as an organizational model. But they merely substitute one form-driven model for another. They fail to recognize that the problems of pyramidal institutions cannot be solved by simply redesigning pyramids.

Success in the 1990s depends on our ability to give up our form-driven paradigm altogether. *Leadership for the 21st century depends on developing a function-driven paradigm.* Rather than debating the merits of one form versus another, we must create a new paradigm that is based on function or purpose. Only after individuals or groups determine their mission can they organize to achieve it. As goals change, structures should be adjusted accordingly.

This new function-driven paradigm derives its power from the fact that it more accurately fits the laws of nature than the old form-driven paradigm. Scientists from every discipline have in recent decades found evidence to refute the Newtonian view of reality. Astronomer James Jeans noted this shift in thinking in 1930 when he declared, "The universe begins to look more like a great thought than like a great machine." Discoveries in quantum physics, chaos theory, and self-organizing systems have led scientists to define reality in terms of relationships rather than in terms of objects. They now recognize that even subatomic particles change their shape depending on their purpose.

The findings of scientists in the biological and physical realms apply to people and organizations as well. If we do not revise our old assumptions, we will never have an accurate understanding of how people and organizations behave. We are so accustomed to thinking of organizations in terms of their structures that it is difficult to imagine them being defined by their purposes and relationships. We want to know, "Who is the ultimate decision maker?" The answer "It all depends" does not satisfy our need for certainty. Nor does it fit with the pyramidal model we have come to know and love/hate. When we ask, "Who reports to whom?" we find another "It all depends" disconcerting. We don't want to have to think in unfamiliar ways, in spite of the fact that our old assumptions and behaviors are not bringing us the success that we want.

However difficult it is to comprehend, the function-driven paradigm more accurately describes reality than the form-driven model. Haven't you ever wondered why people and organizations never seem to behave? Why is it that organizations defy the desires of those who run them? Why do people act as if they have no regard for order and rules — and how do they get away with it? As long as we expect people and organizations to act according to set patterns that do not describe nor predict their behavior, we will be frustrated and confused. Only by developing a function-driven paradigm can we begin to understand how people actually act, individually and in organizations.

A function-driven person or organization is defined by its purpose or mission. Whatever structure or form it takes is designed to best achieve its purpose. Its purpose or mission — its internal integrity — is what defines it as an organization — not its structure or shape.

From a function-driven view, any group of individuals acting as a family would *be* a family, regardless of whether they fit our form-driven image of what a family should be. Likewise, a corporation or government agency might adopt a function-driven approach to training. It would then create learning experiences for its employees so they could develop the knowledge, skills, and perspectives needed. The organization might conclude that the best way to help its employees develop the desired skills is to have them attend classes. Or it may conclude that its employees can best learn by interacting with others in the organization, visiting other organizations, and participating in a host of other educational experiences. Form would follow purpose.

With any organization, be it a family unit of two or a nation of millions, it is vital to the health of the organization that all its members understand and accept its purpose. For this to happen, the free flow of information is essential. Because bureaucracy inhibits the free flow of information and the ability to adjust quickly, function-driven organizations tend to have fewer levels of employees, fewer rules, and less red tape. Like the organs of the body, all parts of the system are connected, gathering information from one another and from the outside environment. This is a far cry from the pyramid, where only those at the bottom have direct contact with the product or customer. A function-driven organization, like a living organism, is interactive with its environment. When one part of it is touched, it responds as a whole, taking in the new information and using it to respond more effectively.

Communication in a function-driven organization is multidirectional instead of top down. Individuals or groups within the organization can communicate directly with any individual or group. This is a significant departure from form-driven organizations, where individual units within the larger organization — mini-pyramids themselves — view other units as competitors from whom useful information must be withheld. Whereas employees in form-driven organizations are always rating their most serious internal problem as "communications," employees in function-driven organizations communicate openly and freely to better perform their functions. Barriers to communication are eliminated through a host of mechanisms.

Of course, function-driven organizations also need to perform administrative tasks. But, unlike the pyramid, lines of communication run in every direction and intersect frequently. Tasks can be managed by one team at one time and by another at another time. Administrative activities as well as communication lines become much more flexible. Specialized units may exist, but they are linked to other units to meet the organization's mission. For example, accounting departments may still exist, but they work closely with other departments to help them determine whether their attention and resources are focused on their stated goals and how they might improve.

In the function-driven organization, cooperative teamwork is rewarded. Collaboration is emphasized over competition. Teams focus on specific tasks and reorganize once those tasks are accomplished. Financial rewards are not based on which individual outperforms others but on how well the group as a whole does at reaching its goals. New partnerships, sometimes among former enemies, become commonplace, as mutual interests take precedence over differences.

Shared decision making and group accomplishments are valued more than individual status, titles, and power. Leadership rotates among group members, depending on tasks involved, time available, and skills required. Task force leaders might be those who have particular expertise or interest in the goal, regardless of their job titles. In different groups, they might play supporting roles as others assume the lead. Leaders are less concerned with making decisions themselves than ensuring that the necessary information and resources are available to decision makers.

In function-driven organizations, there are many different kinds of power, which are shared by different groups of people as well as different individuals. Teams, for example, may be responsible for hiring — and even firing — within their units. Promotions may be determined by one's colleagues. Re-

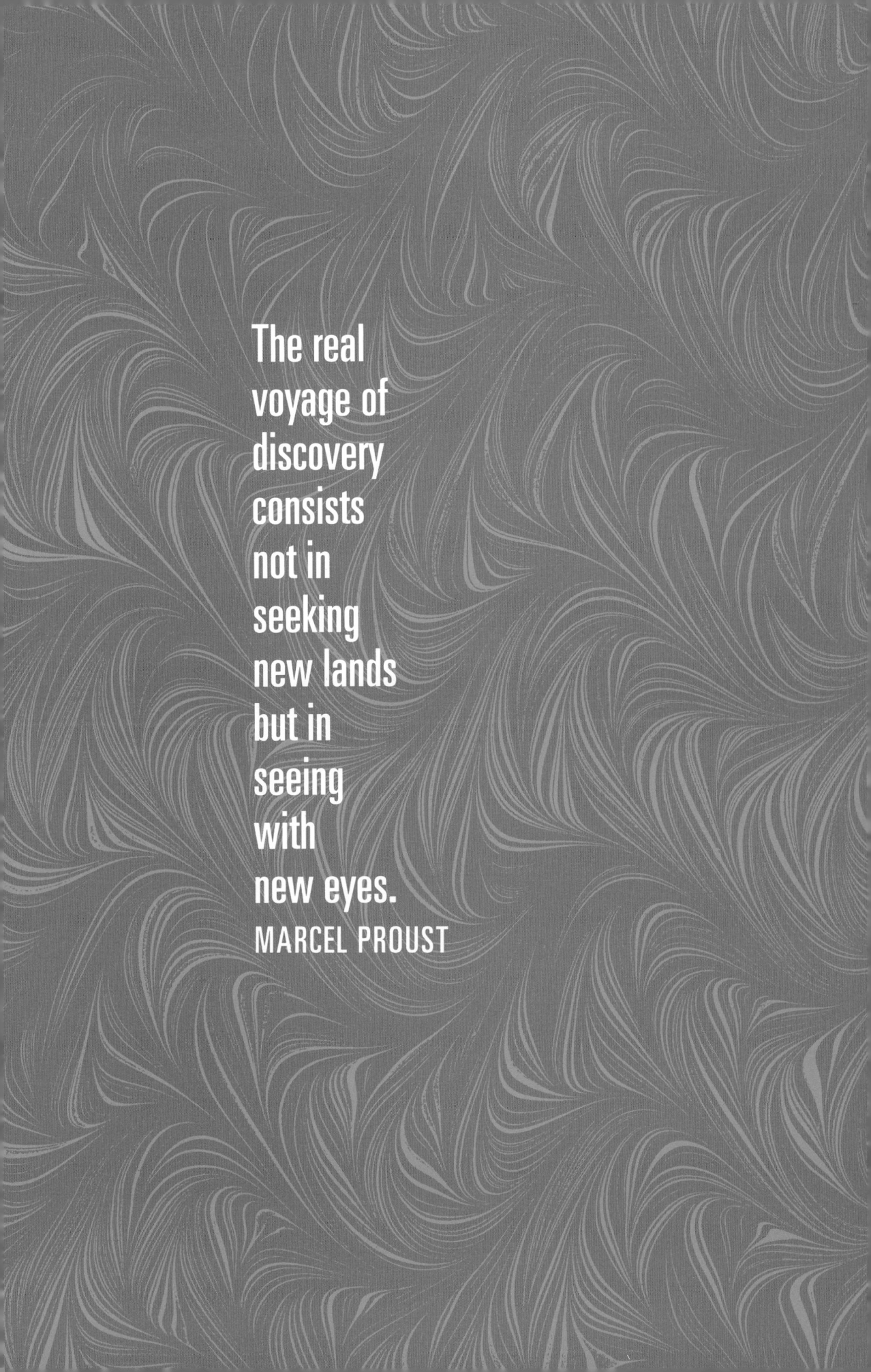

The real voyage of discovery consists not in seeking new lands but in seeing with new eyes.
MARCEL PROUST

porting to those who govern and have fiscal responsibility may be shared so that team leaders may make presentations on the projects they head, regardless of whether they are the "senior" staff member on their team.

Power, then, is not based solely on job titles but is also created through personal or situational influence and the expertise people bring to each problem. Within pyramidal organizations power and influence are considered finite; if one person has more, by definition someone else has less. But in function-driven organizations, power is viewed as infinite. It can be generated by individuals or teams who assume leadership roles, accept responsibility, make decisions, share with others, take risks, and facilitate productive change.

Our beliefs about power come from traditions that were well established before the Industrial Revolution. In fact, the Industrial Age was built on these beliefs about power and control. They were brought to our shores by Calvinists, Puritans, and others who promoted a hierarchical, patriarchal view of the world and saw human nature as essentially evil and human beings in need of salvation (i.e., control). Although these views have become predominant in the 20th century, it is important to note that in our nation's early history many other traditions existed. The Quakers, for example, did not hold this hierarchical, individualistic, authoritarian view of power. Indeed, they believed in shared, consensual decision making, peaceful coexistence within a diverse culture, and other traits of a function-driven paradigm.

Redefining power can help an individual or organization become more function-driven. One of the simplest ways to begin this journey is to share more information with a greater number of people. Because function-driven organizations rely on collaborative problem solving, those within the organization must have the most current, complete, and accurate information available. Therefore, information access, analysis, and synthesis become more important than mere data gathering. When information is shared, artificial walls between departments and people disintegrate. Units and individuals begin to understand that they are all part of the same organization, trying to accomplish a common purpose. They recognize that they all hold valuable puzzle pieces that must fit together. Access to information empowers people, not only enabling them to make better decisions, but also helping them feel like they are an integral part of the organization. Power becomes shared, and rewards can be based on group accomplishments rather than merely on one's location on the organizational chart, as in the form-driven organization.

Function-driven organizations are dynamic. They are

alive. They are *learning* organizations, constantly making changes based on the latest information, adjusting strategic goals and plans, striving to improve services, and finding ways to work smarter. They are flexible, responding quickly to changing environments and conditions in the marketplace. They are able to take in information from any point in the organization and make it instantly available to anyone who needs it, encouraging everyone to make more effective use of it.

Whereas form-driven organizations are tied to the past and resist change, function-driven organizations are future-oriented and welcome change. Risk-taking, experimentation, creativity, and innovation are encouraged because they are considered essential to proactive problem solving in a dynamic world. Teams that generate ideas to improve products or services, work conditions, safety, productivity, morale, profitability, or any other aspect of the organization are rewarded. No artificial boundaries are placed on what employees can tackle.

Quality, not just quantity, is emphasized and becomes everyone's responsibility, not just that of the inspector at the end of the assembly line. Rather than valuing Frederick Taylor's attention to efficiency, function-driven organizations develop philosophies consistent with those of Malcolm Baldrige and W. Edwards Deming, which focus on continuous improvement, employee participation, and organizational effectiveness. Rather than looking for packaged panaceas for their ills, function-driven organizations use external resources and information to solve their own problems internally. This approach, coupled with the capacity to adapt quickly, offers a potential for economic growth unimaginable in the old pyramid-shaped institutions.

Unlike the form-driven organization, which was motivated by the desire for profit and power by the few at the top, the function-driven organization is guided by its mission. It strives to align all activities to achieve its core purpose. There is no room for individual fiefdoms and sacred cows. All projects, policies, structures, and beliefs need to be consistent with the vision and goals of the organization, which are more important than the ego needs or personal peccadilloes of a particular manager.

Function-driven organizations do not attempt to accomplish or assess their purpose in a quarterly reporting period. Their leaders embrace a longer view. They develop long-term business strategies rather than focusing solely on short-term profit. No longer are programs (and common sense) dictated by rigid, short-term, bottom-line considerations. These organizations understand that long-term investments in research, training, new technologies, and safety and health are in their best interest.

In function-driven organizations, workers' concerns are no longer at odds with the concerns of those "at the top" — in fact, there is little concern about who is "on top" because the interests of all individuals within the organization merge. Each individual is valued. Just as the brain cells depend on the lungs, the heart, the blood, and all the other cells, so do all individuals in a function-driven organization have integrity and purpose. Function-driven organizations become responsive to the needs of all their members because their leaders understand that organizational goals can be met only through the active participation of informed, empowered employees at every level.

The importance of employee buy-in was illustrated by a recent visitor to an organization where I was a consultant. Observing their recently formed problem-solving teams he was unable to tell "management" from "labor." He meant this as a criticism. I took it as a compliment. He helped me recognize how much things had changed in a matter of a few months. Only six months before, there were many visible (and, to many employees, annoying) indications that some employees were more valued than others. Now, such barriers to collaboration had vanished. Everyone was dressed in whatever he or she felt was appropriate; job titles did not depend on placing others in subservient roles; everyone was working in problem-solving teams. And, according to their accounts, they were *really* working — some said for the first time. The old lines of demarcation, so evident in the pyramidal structure of the recent past, had become blurred beyond distinction. In fact, structure and its symbols were no longer important to the employees. They were focused on solving mutual problems and keeping their company alive. I knew they had truly internalized a new organizational culture when I entered a work area and observed one former "hard-line" manager deeply engrossed in the time-management issue his team was tackling. He had volunteered to serve as recorder for this particular session, while the group was being dynamically facilitated by a young woman who only months before had been a trainee in his department!

Leaders in function-driven organizations are developing innovative evaluation methods that measure results thought to be unmeasurable in the pyramid. And they are focusing on results, not just on superficial impressions. Whereas employees in form-driven organizations would often be punished if they were late for work or challenged their boss, workers in function-driven organizations are trusted as valuable members of their teams. The quality of their work is a measure of their value — not whether they punched in and out at the appropriate times or whether their boss likes their personality.

Additionally, function-driven organizations have abandoned the obsolete notion that everything important is quantifiable and only the quantifiable is important. They are not burdened by a mass of statistics as the only way to determine whether their goals are being met. Instead, they use a wide range of evaluation techniques that provide a broader and deeper picture of their progress. They seek information that is accurate and current, regardless of whether it is flattering. Whereas the pyramidal value system encouraged only data that supported existing assumptions and biases, those in function-driven organizations attempt to gather as much valuable information as possible. Only by having a complete picture, however painful or uncomfortable, can they make the wisest decisions. They understand that the very act of observing or measuring affects outcome and therefore recognize that *what* is measured and *how* it is measured must be tied to purpose and not left to chance.

The function-driven organization also places ethics at its very core. In fact, many function-driven organizations strive to identify and achieve a "highest calling," the single most important thing they can do that others may not be able to do. They consider this to be what makes them unique. In addition, function-driven organizations clean up their environmental messes, police their own industries, and invest in education, research, and public service. They expect ethical behavior from their employees as well as themselves. They understand that doing the right thing also makes good economic sense.

Function-driven organizations understand that they are linked in numerous ways to other systems, larger and smaller, worldwide. Unlike the slow-to-react "dinosaur" organizations that are form-driven, function-driven organizations have nervous systems that are sensitive and responsive. Touch them anywhere and you touch them everywhere, including all the other systems to which they are connected.

Leaders of function-driven organizations profoundly understand this connectedness. They take responsibility for social, environmental, economic, and other problems their organizations may create. They consider how their behaviors will affect others, now and in future generations. The form-driven paradigm promoted the belief that civic and ethical responsibilities are incompatible with profit — a belief that is being proven wrong by a host of very profitable and ethical function-driven organizations, which are described in the next section.

Function-driven thinkers take a more holistic approach to issues. For example, a function-driven view of health care incorporates an appreciation of physical, emotional, and spiritual well-being. It addresses prevention of illness, not just treatment of diseases. A function-driven reform process emphasizes collaborative efforts that value the needs and interests of everyone, not just the special interests of those with the most resources.

The integrated approach of the function-driven paradigm can be applied in all areas of society. A commitment to public safety replaces the negative focus on crime, and public safety involves all citizens — entire neighborhoods of residents, shopkeepers, business owners, and employees — in creating safe, secure communities. Function-driven religious institutions focus more on meeting the spiritual needs of their members or community and less on generating income to perpetuate the status quo. In function-driven education systems, learning is at the core of all activities. Students are not simply taught isolated bits of knowledge, leaving to chance their ability to coherently assemble random "factoids." They share responsibility with parents, community, and educators for learning an integrated set of skills, perspectives, and information that will help them become productive, happy adults.

In a function-driven society, every individual is respected for his or her intrinsic worth; our value to others is not defined by our job title. We may have many jobs, roles, tasks, avocations, and civic responsibilities — all of which are important aspects of who we are, but none of which defines us. Who we are is defined by each of us through the purpose we claim and act out in our day-to-day activities and interactions.

CHAPTER NINE

Styles of Managing Change

The decade ahead is our entryway into a new millennium. As we enter it, the inability of the form-driven paradigm to address our personal, organizational, and societal needs will become more evident. Even now form-driven organizations are coming under increased scrutiny because they simply cannot keep up with new technologies and new realities. As complex, interconnected issues emerge all over the world, form-driven institutions are being summoned to cope with them. They increasingly fail. Too often they do more harm than good, becoming more a part of the problem than a source of its solutions.

The solutions to welfare, education, unemployment, crime, and pollution problems are beyond the capacity of form-driven institutions. In the field of health care, for example, pyramidal institutions have increasingly resisted innovations that could improve health care for millions, forcing the federal government, by popular mandate, to intervene. Many religious institutions refuse to reexamine their established positions on a host of issues, in spite of the changes that have occurred in society. Our legal and justice systems resist change, in spite of the fact that in this century more Americans have been murdered in peacetime than have died in wars.

It is not just our inability to move forward that is worrisome; our form-driven institutions are unable to provide us with the quality of life we enjoyed in the recent past. The effects touch all of us. Our cities struggle more than ever. Our infrastructure is beginning to collapse, and transportation systems are failing to keep up with contemporary needs. Hardly a family has been untouched by unemployment and health care concerns. Every city in the country is grappling with the problem of homeless families. Pollution has become a fact of life.

Because of this widening gap between what is required of our institutions and what they deliver, an increasing number of people are losing confidence in such form-driven fields as medicine, law, politics, banking, and government. This distrust of traditional pyramidal institutions and their representatives certainly contributed to the tremendous appeal that H. Ross Perot had for many voters in the election of 1992.

A recent study conducted by pollsters James Patterson and Peter Kim explored the confidence Americans have in their traditional institutions. It found that only about one in three Americans accepted without question the moral guidance of religious institutions or their leaders. The Supreme Court commanded the confidence of 25 percent, and the president of the United States lagged well behind the nine justices with only 19 percent. Local politicians were far down the list at 6 percent. School teachers and college professors were considered moral authorities by 23 percent and 20 percent, respectively. The American press, much esteemed when reporters were uncovering the Watergate scandals, was rated at 6 percent — only 1 percent better than fictional television characters!

Although people are disillusioned with traditional institutions, they still want to hope for a better future. The quality of the future we build is linked with our attitudes toward change. In one way or another, change is threatening and uncomfortable for everyone. Preserving personal traditions and resisting fleeting trends or social conventions may not be harmful. But resisting fundamental change is devastating for individuals, organizations, and society. There are four distinct responses to change, each with its own unique costs and benefits. Let's examine each briefly.

Deniers

Deniers, just as their name implies, reject the notion that the world is changing in any meaningful way. Most of them do not acknowledge today's dramatic technological, social, economic, and political shifts as any departure from the past. Other Deniers reluctantly acknowledge some changes but dismiss them as inconsequential, subscribing to the slogan, "The more things change, the more they remain the same."

Because they believe the future will be very similar to the past, Deniers feel justified in clinging to their pyramidal view of the world. In fact, many of them go so far as to blame the problems confronting society on those who want to deviate from pyramidal norms and structures. They insist that we would have fewer problems today if only everyone would hold form-driven values and behave in form-driven patterns.

There have always been Deniers, and they have often been influential, although their views seem almost comical when scrutinized from an historical perspective. It is hard to believe that Deniers were so persuasive in their times. For example, King Ferdinand and Queen Isabella of Spain organized a powerful committee in 1486 to study Columbus's plan to find a shorter route to the Indies. It concluded:

1. A voyage to Asia would require three years.
2. The Western Ocean is infinite and perhaps unnavigable.
3. If Columbus reached the Antipodes (the land on the other side of the globe from Europe), he could not get back.
4. There are no Antipodes because the greater part of the globe is covered with water and because St. Augustine says so.
5. Of the five zones, only three are habitable.
6. So many centuries after the Creation, it is unlikely that anyone could find hitherto unknown lands of any value.

Another example is the Roman Catholic Church's treatment of the 17th-century Italian mathematician, astronomer, and physicist Galileo Galilei. The first person to use a telescope and one of history's greatest scientists, Galileo was forced by the Roman Inquisition to recant his scientific theories and spend the last eight years of his life under house arrest — because he believed that the earth revolved around the sun. His judges feared that if his ideas were taught, they would undermine Catholic tradition at a time it was under attack by Protestant reformers. Only in 1992, after a 13-year study, did a church commission find Galileo not guilty of heresy. Three hundred fifty-nine years after the Church denied Galileo's findings, the Pope himself attended the proceedings to make it official: the earth *does* revolve around the sun.

Today, individuals, organizations, and even nations fall into the Denier camp. Like Deniers of the past, they cling to outmoded images of a world that no longer exists. Deniers are found among corporate giants, education administrators, religious leaders, and government officials. They are easily identified by their steadfast devotion to old systems, structures, and solutions. These have led to success in the past and, Deniers insist, will surely carry us successfully into the future.

Of course, the benefit of being a Denier is the supreme confidence that one has all the answers, answers that rarely have to be reexamined or reformulated. Being able to block out change and the need to adapt to it leads to comfort, if not self-righteousness. We have all seen elderly people whose manner suggests that in their minds they are still living in the time of their youth. Such people seem happy with themselves, if out of touch with reality. So too are Deniers happy with themselves — until the realities of the external world come crashing in on them.

Many Denier businesses have discovered — often too late — that they were in serious danger because they refused to notice external forces. Henry Ford, for example, failed to anticipate the effect veterans with greater disposable incomes returning from World War I would have on the auto industry. Until that time, Ford had been the industry leader by offering a car "in any color, as long as it's black." A victim of his own success, he refused to add additional paint colors — only to fall behind General Motors, which recognized societal changes and their implications.

Many current examples of Deniers can be found in the business section of any daily newspaper. Many pyramidal organizations, once believed to be immune from setbacks and layoffs, are being forced to reexamine their assumptions and alter their behaviors.

One cannot be a Denier forever. The cost of being a Denier is that sooner or later the world will pass you by because change is inevitable. With global communications networks, the fast pace of change, and the increased demands being placed on individuals and organizations alike, Deniers have as much chance of continuing to live in their comfortable, make-believe world as ostriches have of surviving a tidal wave by burying their heads deeper in the sand.

Resisters

Resisters grudgingly acknowledge that changes are occurring and that these changes require different attitudes and behaviors, but they make only the most minimal adaptations — and then only when absolutely necessary. Resisters wish things could remain as they are — or better yet return to the way they were. They sadly concede that times are changing and that they will have to sacrifice the comfortable norms and patterns of the past.

Resisters are psychological foot-draggers. They want to hold onto their pyramidal view of the world and are reluctant to incorporate into their frame of reference anything that might conflict with their pyramidal assumptions. For example, Resisters are reluctant to use new technologies. Whereas Deniers will refuse to have advanced technologies around them, Resisters may have a computer on their desk but will not use it.

The advantage of being a Resister is the feeling of safety that this point of view engenders. Resisters are never too far out in front — yet they can assure themselves that they are more open to change than Deniers. Resisters take only the most measured risks, so although they rarely have dramatic successes, they often manage to scrape by — which is often their ultimate goal.

Resister organizations, like individuals, often wait until the last moment to make changes in their structures, policies, practices, and technologies. Sometimes they wait too long or make insufficient changes. In any case, Resister organizations are common today. Their leaders dismiss as fads many new ideas that could improve their productivity and effectiveness. Whatever changes they do make are often piecemeal and insignificant, leaving the core of their business untouched.

The costs of being a Resister can be tremendous. Resister individuals not only hold themselves back, they also injure those around them. Resister parents hamper their children's development. Resister doctors endanger their patients' health. Resister bosses restrict the effectiveness of their employees.

Because they reinforce the status quo and discourage change, Resister institutions have organizational cultures that encourage employees to focus on what *cannot* be done rather than what *can* be done. Many government, educational, and other nonprofit groups are great Resisters. They deviate from the pyramid only when they have to. The pyramidal philosophy so permeates some organizations that members cannot detect their own resistant attitudes. They accept the beliefs of the pyramid that encourage resistance. They resist sharing responsibility because they believe that employees are essentially not trustworthy. They resist sharing information because internal competition is fierce. They resist efforts to improve because mediocrity is the norm. Collaboration is tolerated only when it is financially required and only for as long as necessary. New ideas are resisted in numerous clever ways and ultimately are squelched or simply ignored.

Senior executives in Resister organizations sometimes concede privately that if they really want to get important tasks done well and quickly, they must circumvent their own bureaucracy. Unwilling to alter the basic pyramidal structure of their organizations, these leaders establish problem-solving task forces to work outside of the pyramid. They then strive to maintain control of both the pyramid and the alternative structures they have created.

Such task forces can be effective when they are part of a larger commitment to restructure an entire organization, but they usually fail when they are attempted by Resister organizations. There is often a great deal of confusion about how the work done outside the pyramid by independent task forces fits back into the structure. Sometimes such work (if there is any) is not even intended to fit back in — the only purpose of the task force is to demonstrate to various interest groups that their concerns are being considered. One certain effect is that employees still operating in the pyramid become even more demoralized and cynical.

Those perched at the top of pyramids are not the only ones resistant to change. Many people are satisfied with the pyramidal structure; they know and accept the rules of the game. Many Americans, comfortable with form-driven institutions' abilities and inabilities, expect little of them. In spite of some complaining, they are satisfied with the status quo. For example, in virtually every major poll, the majority of American parents express the belief that American education is in trouble. However, when asked about their children's *own* schools, they express satisfaction. American students perform at lower levels than Japanese and European students, yet American parents still express greater satisfaction with their schools than do their counterparts in Japan and Europe.

Similarly, many Americans voice great distress with elected politicians. But we keep voting the same politicians into office or, worse, permit them to be reelected by not voting at all. Polls consistently report Americans' unhappiness with Congress as an institution, yet we continue to support our own representatives. Ironically, in 1992 voters in 14 states demanded term limitations while returning their incumbents to office!

The halls of Congress are, in fact, a place to find prime examples of Resisters. Many candidates advocate change when they are up for reelection, only to vote against anything that might make their constituents uncomfortable in the short term. They want to cut military spending — but not when it means closing military bases in their districts. They want to cut farm subsidies — until it affects their voters. They speak about improving education or health care — but will act only if they are sure they will not be hurting their chances for reelection.

The same resistance to change and fear of the unknown is seen at the international level. In Russia and Eastern

Europe, for instance, there is a strong movement to return to the security and predictability of communism. Many who say they suffered greatly under communist regimes are now supporting measures to return in that direction because the known, however unpleasant, feels better to them than the unknown.

Pretenders

Pretenders take a third approach to addressing contemporary change. Pretenders espouse the values of the function-driven paradigm but act on the values of the pyramid. In an effort to appear modern or futuristic, they pick up the language of those trying to transform organizational structures. Through reading, attending conferences, and associating with visionary leaders, they acquire the vocabulary of real "change agents." Yet they consistently fail to practice what they preach.

Pretenders may be the most confusing and dangerous of those who represent the four views toward change because they appear to be one thing but are indeed another. Pretenders talk about trust and cooperation, while their communication and reward systems foster distrust and competition. Pretenders may say they value risk-taking, but they often punish it if it does not produce the results they desire. They may say they value ethical choices, but beware if such choices jeopardize short-term profits!

Sometimes Pretenders are consciously deceptive, believing that others will not catch on. All too often their actions do not live up to their words because they are trapped in their old views without knowing it. They express philosophies they may comprehend or even embrace intellectually but are unable or unwilling to put their ideas into action. Though Pretenders often deceive themselves, they rarely deceive those who work for them. Tragically, millions of people are trapped in Pretender organizations today and feel powerless to change the organization's dynamics.

If there is something positive about being a Pretender, it is that at least they say the right words. Because of this, Pretenders can sometimes be embarrassed, coaxed, or forced into aligning their behavior with their rhetoric. Pretender organizations that say they value long-term, global thinking have a greater likelihood of being encouraged to reward such behaviors than Denier or Resister organizations. Pretenders that claim to be equal opportunity employers but discriminate or tolerate harassment have been stopped in their tracks by lawsuits, prompting them to comply with their rhetoric — and the law.

For short periods of time and at a great distance, Pretenders can look impressive. They have fooled many an employee, investor, and award-giver. If Pretenders believe their own rhetoric, they also develop a false sense of pride in their progressiveness, and often exude a sense of self-satisfaction about how "with it" they are.

Pretender organizations frequently experiment with the latest management trends, but always do so without challenging their pyramidal structures. They pay lip service to strategic planning, quality circles, Total Quality Management (TQM), and a bevy of other processes that could be transformative, but without genuine commitment at the top, their efforts at change are destined to fail. Pretender individuals and organizations end up only reinforcing the status quo and further frustrating employees hungry for real change.

The disadvantage of being a Pretender is that one is living a lie that sooner or later becomes exposed. Often others see through Pretenders' hypocrisy before they realize their own self-deception. The damage done by pretending is often unimaginable. Pretender individuals and organizations continually confuse people who must grapple with the frustration of sorting out mixed messages. The scars on employees caused by working in Pretender organizations are deep and long-lasting. The mistrust and cynicism caused by Pretenders is hard to overcome. When an organization makes a real commitment to realignment, workers who have been damaged by Pretender employers simply will not believe it and will refuse to participate.

Embracers

Embracers expect, even welcome, change. They are secure enough to know that change is never easy and that adjusting to external changes in our environment is simply part of growing. They accept uncertainty and ambiguity as natural and learn to live with unknowns in their lives. They push through their fears by taking risks and trusting themselves, others, and the process of growing.

Organizations and people who *embrace* change were described earlier as Navigators. They understand that change in their external world requires commensurate changes in their own attitudes and behaviors. They recognize that the pyramidal model is becoming increasingly dysfunctional and embrace alternative ways of organizing. Embracer individuals are attracted to one another and will find each other in a crowd, almost as if they have radar to help them locate kindred spirits. Embracer organizations likewise seek collaborators, clients, and customers who share their view of change. Although Embracers are not popular with Deniers and Resisters, they are attractive to Pretenders, who want to be seen with them but do not want them to get too close for fear of being found out.

Some individuals and organizations are "born" with a secure, open, adventurous nature and naturally adopt the function-driven paradigm. In the 1960s, I worked in such an organization. This small manufacturing firm had never used time clocks; it encouraged employees to work in teams and share responsibility for quality. The company was guided by its mission and pride in doing what it did well rather than being directed by an organizational chart. I remember experienced employees telling me when I arrived to think like the customer. We did, and the business thrived. When we had a good year, everyone benefited. When we had a lean year, we decided collectively how to trim expenses. Some employees whose incomes were not as essential to their families offered to reduce their hours so that primary breadwinners would not suffer as much.

Managers were always available to us for consultation and wanted us to be problem solvers. We learned as many different tasks as possible and freely rotated jobs. Cost-cutting solutions or innovative suggestions were usually implemented and rewarded. In the ensuing years, one after another of this company's customers took their business to foreign competition. Yet in spite of market forces that caused its domestic competitors to close their doors, the company reinvented itself several times, each time moving to a new product or industry at the right moment. It continues to thrive because it still operates on the forward-looking, participatory philosophy on which it was founded — in spite of the fact that its primary product today was not even conceived of five years ago!

Function-driven organizations exist today in international partnerships, community-based projects, corporate ventures, and government and nonprofit initiatives. In some instances, new organizations are emerging in response to market niches created when form-driven organizations failed to meet the changing needs of consumers or clients. In other cases, existing organizations are successfully transforming themselves from the old to the new paradigm by changing their beliefs, their reward systems, the kind of employees they hire and promote, and the very way they manage and do business. As a result, their forms or structures are also changing.

Embracer organizations are not only doing the same things differently — they are doing different things. For example, many are treating their employees as valuable assets rather than as expendable resources. They are designing innovative human resource policies to help employees balance work, family, and other responsibilities. Many have contributed money and space for child-care centers at work locations. Seven well-known companies recently teamed up to place child-care workers in the homes of employees whose usual child-care arrangements fell through. Other companies are allowing managers to work flexible schedules. One of the nation's largest banks allows employees at all levels to reduce time and job commitments to care for dependents without cutting off advancement opportunities.

Embracers know how difficult it is to abandon the form-driven paradigm, but they understand that the stakes are high and that it must be done. The benefit of being an Embracer is the satisfaction that results from tackling tough problems, searching for fresh solutions, improving effectiveness, and charting new courses of action. Embracers have a creative energy; they are risk-takers, adventurers. They may have the same fears as others do about change, but they have the courage to overcome their fears and try new things. They may struggle with the changes that are required of them, but they do not quit or back away. Their commitment is to something larger than themselves, which fortifies them in working through their discomfort. *Embracers believe that the cost of not changing is greater than the cost of changing.*

One of the disadvantages of being an Embracer is that one can get too far ahead of others and thus become ineffective or even risk being sacrificed by an organization or society that retrenches. Embracer organizations can try to make too many changes too quickly — although many Resister and Pretender organizations use this as an excuse for retrenching. Embracers are also frequently misunderstood. Throughout history, Embracers have been misinterpreted by their contemporaries, their insights and wisdom appreciated only after they had arduously paved the way and moved on.

The longer our economic, political, social, and religious institutions cling to the form-driven paradigm, the wider the gap becomes between the problems we face and our ability to address them. If we are to thrive individually, organizationally, nationally, and globally, we need to embrace a function-driven paradigm so that we can meet the challenges — and seize the opportunities — of the 21st century. The next section describes some of the key traits of individuals and organizations that have embraced change and are guided by the function-driven paradigm.

SECTION 3

Managing Change: The 21st-Century Leadership Challenge

MYTH #3: **There Is Nothing We Can Do to Influence the Future.**

Several assumptions underlie this third dangerous myth. First of all, the myth is based on the widely held assumption that most people do not make a difference — that only those few at the top of the pyramid are leaders who shape history. Second, it suggests that, since we cannot know what the future holds, we cannot prepare for it or influence it. Nothing could be further from the truth.

Leadership is not a commodity that comes with a job title. It can be exerted by anyone at any time who has a vision for the future and works to realize that vision. And we do not need to know how the future will unfold before taking action. Although we may not know what the future holds for any of us, we can observe that there are people and organizations who are managing today's changes productively and constructively. We can identify the skills and abilities that make them successful and learn to develop and apply these same skills.

Reformers who cling to the form-driven paradigm believe that there are objective truths and universal answers that can be studied, quantified, and transferred from one individual, organization, or nation to another. They are convinced that successful programs can be packaged and sold to other interested parties.

Those who are moving to a function-driven paradigm are recognizing that reality is more subjective and less predictable than we had believed. We cannot import solutions from other communities or organizations and expect to successfully graft them onto our own. The new sciences suggest that solutions are dynamic and homegrown rather than static and imposed from the outside. Effective changes may be informed by others' successes, but they must be developed by those who implement them and implemented in accordance with principles that govern the behavior patterns of organic and inorganic matter.

During more than 20 years of working with government, business, and public sector leaders, I have studied the behavior of thousands of individuals and organizations who are — and are not — effective in a rapidly changing environment. It seems that certain individuals and organizations have developed a toolkit for the 21st century, a set of skills and perspectives that enable them to successfully handle the unexpected while charting a course toward their goals. These effective leaders exhibit seven common characteristics. Those behaviors are (1) building a long-term, global perspective, (2) concentrating on quality and service, (3) encouraging innovation and flexibility, (4) improving cooperation and communication, (5) committing to ethical practices, (6) exercising empowerment, and (7) being propelled by purpose.

Leaders who are effective in managing change exhibit these traits. The more individuals and organizations display one of these traits, the more likely they are to demonstrate the others. In spite of coming from different backgrounds and representing different fields, successful leaders share remarkably similar beliefs and actions.

Whether they direct a large or small organization — or none at all, whether they are in business, government, the arts, education, or any other field, those who are effectively managing change have something to offer the rest of us. Their actions provide a model of what it takes to be an effective leader through the 1990s and into the 21st century.

This section of the book describes the behaviors that help these leaders manage change, solve complex problems, increase organizational effectiveness, and improve personal satisfaction. This section shows the range of styles in which function-driven leadership can be developed. The stories retold here also illustrate that leaders adopt these behaviors in line with their own personal styles and the needs of their organizations. Thus, although many lessons can be learned from the leaders described in this section, each of us must forge our own unique path to achieve our goals.

CHAPTER TEN

Building a Long-Term, Global Perspective

*"I*n our every deliberation we must consider the impact of our decisions on the next seven generations," states the seventh-generation test of the Iroquois and Mohawk tribes. These tribes believe that they will make wiser choices if they consider the consequences of their actions far into the future.

By sharp contrast, most of us rarely consider the long-term consequences of our actions — not for seven generations, rarely for seven months. In fact, we often do not worry about the consequences of our actions at all. And if we do, our concerns are usually immediate and personal. We rarely consider the effect our actions might have on others in the future. This is also true with organizations. In spite of management by objectives, computer technologies, megatrend monitoring, and endless analysis of flowcharts, graphs, and histograms, too many of our decisions are made to satisfy the decision makers rather than the long-term needs of all stakeholders.

To illustrate this to yourself, examine your thoughts to see how long term and global they are. For a day, record your thoughts or activities at the turn of every hour on a time-space chart like the one that follows. The horizontal axis represents time, while the vertical axis represents space, or the contexts in which you live your life. If you are like most people, the majority of your concerns over the course of a day (and week, year, and lifetime) will be in the bottom left-hand corner, representing personal, short-term issues.

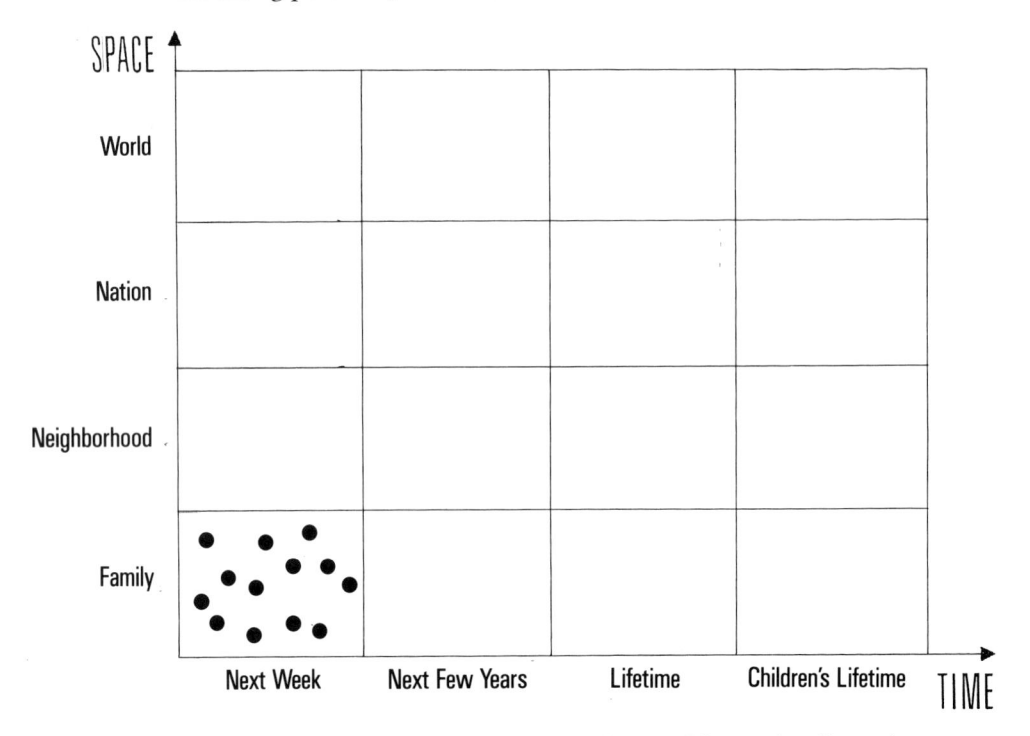

[Chart: A time-space grid. Vertical axis labeled SPACE with rows Family, Neighborhood, Nation, World. Horizontal axis labeled TIME with columns Next Week, Next Few Years, Lifetime, Children's Lifetime. Dots cluster in the Family / Next Week cell.]

In the past, we may have been able to dwell in the here and now with few negative consequences. Planning may not have been essential to our survival. Today's world, however, is very different. The impact of our actions on others is greater than it was in the past. And with modern technological links and a global economy, a greater number of people are affected by our actions than in previous eras. This requires that individuals and organizations that want to lead develop the ability to assess the long-term and global as well as short-term and immediate effects of their actions. This ability is like having a zoom lens on a camera that can be adjusted as needed.

A long-term, global perspective does not require that we stop thinking about short-term considerations that touch those nearest us; it means that our concerns need to be expanded. We will always need to address the immediate challenges of day-to-day living: how to get to work in the morning when our usual route is blocked, how to deal with a boss who is having a bad day, how to cope with a sick child, how to get a report finished with incomplete data and a ringing phone. But, increasingly, leaders are extending their thinking into the other blocks of the time-space chart above. They are asking questions like, "If I keep doing things this way, what might the long-term consequences be for me? For others? What are some possible alternative courses of action — and are they likely to produce better results?" "What if I do not want to be in this job/marriage/neighborhood in five years? What steps could I be taking now that will lead me toward a better future?" "Is our business going to be as strong as we'd like it to be in the future? What alternatives could we choose now to ensure its future success? What are the potential consequences of our current course of action? What solutions might we implement, and what might their consequences be?"

C. Van der Klugt, former president of N.V. Philips, the light bulb manufacturer, describes the quality of possessing a long-term, global perspective as being "future-oriented":

> Tomorrow's managers and technicians will need to be right for today — ready for tomorrow. They should be able to analyze the present situation and base conclusions upon that analysis. They must also have knowledge of things to come, the future problems and threats, the possibilities and challenges. In short, they will need the basic skills to become strategic thinkers.

Unless we examine our personal, professional, and civic decisions in light of long-term, global consequences, we can never break free of pyramid-bound thinking. We will be prisoners of short-term demands on our time and energy and never attain long-term goals. We will be unable to alter our old habits to ensure a quality of life that will support future generations.

An anticipatory, long-term perspective can help us avoid the pitfalls we may fear. It can also be used to realize the positive goals we want to accomplish: "We are very happy in our home now, but I can imagine that our life will be changing over the next few years, and we may want to start preparing now for a move." "What if I accomplish one extra task each week for the next six months to show my manager that I deserve a promotion?" "Our American customers love our products. Might we have viable markets in other parts of the world?" "If our community were to institute a ride-share commuter program, how much energy and road wear-and-tear could we save in a decade?"

It is more difficult for Americans than for many other people to think in the long term. As part of the "New World," we have always had new frontiers before us and seemingly unlimited possibilities. In the past, Americans could develop, even deplete, the resources at one location and move on to the next. We did not need to develop a tradition of conserving water, trees, and land as have generations of Europeans. I learned this difference as a child, when a European-born neighbor instructed me to turn off the faucet while brushing my teeth so as not to waste water. She went on to teach me many energy-saving steps that she had learned growing up in a culture more environmentally conscious than ours.

Many other cultures have also historically taken a longer-term view than have Americans. Whereas they might define a long period of time in terms of hundreds or thousands of years, most Americans would define it as a school year or a financial quarter. From building codes to terms of office for elected officials, many aspects of our society reinforce short-term thinking. What incentive is there for elected politicians to try to resolve long-term problems when their terms of office are limited and when reelection depends on making things look good in the short term?

Not only do we need to extend our thinking about time, we need to expand it beyond narrow personal and geographic boundaries. Too many Americans have little knowledge or interest in world affairs. Leaders of pyramid-like institutions too often become internally focused and miss the big picture. Steven Reinemund, vice president and chief executive officer of Frito-Lay, claims that a broad perspective — being able to keep in touch with the world around us — is one of the most important characteristics organizational leaders can have. He says:

It is dangerous when you develop your own lingo, attitudes, and internal perspective — the outside world starts to be viewed as an unnecessary intrusion. We try to apply the "Rose Bowl test": How would this marketing strategy be viewed, not in the comfort of our internal meetings, but on the 50-yard line of the Rose Bowl before 100,000 people? You cannot answer that unless you're connected to the outside world.

Reinemund's view that we must expand our perspective to include a broader context for decision making is shared by successful leaders in every field. They recognize that our world is increasingly global, often in ways we do not even realize. On any given day, employees of Saztec Philippines, an international data entry firm, can be found keying in patient records for hospitals in California and North Carolina, consumer credit reports on British citizens, names and addresses of Stride Rite Shoe clients in the United States, switching networks for the Mountain Bell and Pacific Bell telephone systems, articles in *Playboy* and the *Christian Science Monitor*, U.S. presidential speeches, French novels, European patent records, and the Helsinki, Finland, National Library book catalogue.

Today, more students are studying English in China than in the United States. There are more teachers of English in the former Soviet Union than there are students of Russian in America. A few years ago, the award for best teacher in America went to Bolivian-born Jaime Escalante, whose story was dramatized in the film *Stand and Deliver* and whom President Clinton identified as the American educator he most admired. That same year, the National Spelling Bee, sponsored by the Scripps-Howard newspaper chain, was won by a girl whose name most Americans could not spell: Rageshree Ramachandran; the runner-up was Victor Wang. The world of sports is also more globally interconnected as demonstrated by Olympic athletes who train in or represent countries other than those they were born in.

The television personality with perhaps the world's largest audience lives in the United States yet is virtually unknown in America. Yue-Sai-Kan, a New Yorker born in Guilin, China, hosts and produces a documentary series, *One World,* in the United States and on location, bringing a glimpse of the outside world each week to 300 million Chinese. Thousands of entertainers, musicians, dancers, authors, filmmakers, painters, playwrights, and craftsmen help span national boundaries. And, with cable television, we can experience distant concerts (or wars) as they occur.

Today, long-term, global thinking is not a luxury, it is essential. A good example can be found in the Pacific Northwest, where paper factories that had been shut down for years are being reopened and run at a profit by new owners with a longer-term perspetive. When taking control, the new owners accepted labor unions, local norms, and the existing work force. They changed only one element: the perspective on timing for showing a profit. The previous owners had decided these factories were no longer productive enough to turn a profit. The new owners, however, made a long-term commitment. They let it be known that they expected the factories to be viable — and profitable — down the road. The effect of this perspective was that productivity soared, even in the short run.

Many American businesses are catching on to the value of taking a long-term, global view. In fact, some recent studies conclude that thinking globally is becoming the norm in American business, not the exception.

A survey conducted by the National Association of Manufacturers of small firms shows that two-thirds have some export sales. And corporate recruiters report that experience in overseas sales has now become a prerequisite for top corporate positions. The fact that the chief executives of all three of the big U.S. automakers made their reputations running European divisions is evidence of this.

A long-term, global perspective provides the ability to recognize links among seemingly unrelated data and events. As we stretch our perspective, we begin to identify relationships very unlike the neatly numbered, linear, cause-and-effect connections that our pyramid-oriented schools taught us to look for. This recognition helps us be more systematic and anticipatory in our thinking, interpret events more accurately, and make better decisions.

Long-term, global thinking enables us to size up situations and act more expeditiously than traditional thinking. Furthermore, long-term, global thinkers develop the ability to make decisions in an ambiguous environment. As a result, the unknowns become less scary, and we become more comfortable and assertive because we are more confident of making better decisions.

In a recent interview, Dona Wolf, director of the Human Resources Development Group at the Office of Personnel Management of the federal government, shared her insights into the importance of a long-term, global perspective in the federal government:

As conditions change, people have to change. What we're trying to do is reinvigorate government. It used to be that, in the federal government, we hired people who already had skills we needed, and they just used those specific skills until they retired.

Today, however, there is too much change for us to hire a person for a job. We must hire all employees for a career of government service. And it means investing in those who may have been hired years ago for a specific job but whose employers may not have seen it necessary to expand their skills and give them increased opportunities. Therefore, we need people who want to learn — people who *embrace change.*

Managers have to be comfortable with change — and must create an environment in which change is welcome. The whole nature of management is going to change, from hierarchical and dogmatic to more open communications and team-building.

Wolf reported the results of a recent study of leadership skills for the federal workplace. It concludes that, in addition to the skills needed for lower levels of management, the two skills needed for leadership by senior executives are "vision" and "external awareness." These are what leaders exhibit when they extend their thinking from the bottom left-hand corner of the time-space chart on page 84. When individuals and organizations expand their perspective to include a broader context of time and space dimensions, they are exhibiting vision and external awareness as in the right-hand column.

Function-driven leadership requires moving away from micro-thinking by developing a zoom lens that can look at the long term and global as well as the short term and immediate. The checklist on the next page, which applies to both individuals and organizations, contrasts the characteristics of form-driven, micro-thinking with function-driven, zoom-lens thinking.

Form-Driven Micro-Thinking	**Function-Driven Zoom-Lens Thinking**
Short-term orientation	Long-term and short-term orientation
Focus only on immediate, visible results	Focus on both immediate, visible, measurable results and results that may be invisible and difficult to measure in the short term
Belief in linear, cause-and-effect thinking in which a single issue can easily be identified	Belief in systems thinking, with multiple, and sometimes immeasurable, causes or effects
Analysis based on formulas and procedures	Analysis carried out both systematically and intuitively
Orientation to the past (What worked?)	Orientation to the future and the past (What might work?)
Adaptive	Innovative
Centralized decision making	Decentralized decision making
Focus on isolated data	Focus on context and patterns of data
Inability to respond to crises	Ability to respond to crises quickly
Hoarding information	Sharing information

An increasing number of individuals and organizational leaders are working on practicing the long-term, globally oriented thinking in the column on the right. As they are discovering, this is not as easy as it appears, because they often interact with those who are still operating out of the form-based paradigm. For example, a corporation may want to make long-term investments that its stockholders do not appreciate. A senior government official may encourage global thinking, but her employees may need training, practice, and incentives to put it into practice. A school may want to expand its methods of assessment but may encounter resistance from parents who find percentiles and class standings easier to grasp and a source of status.

Few individuals or organizations are exclusively form- or function-driven. Most display a range of behaviors between the two. Those who want to strengthen their leadership capacity for the future need to identify and reward others who exhibit function-driven leadership. By doing so they not only honor these individuals, they also send a clear message to others about what they value and expect from them. It is in the interest of organizations to develop a long-term, global perspective along with other function-driven leadership traits in all of its employees. After all, organizations cannot be forward thinking if the people who comprise them are not.

Although few workplaces encourage it, a long-term, global perspective can be learned. Using techniques such as futures wheels, brainstorming, trend analysis, scenario writing, contingency planning, vision-building, and a host of other simple methods, anybody can learn to develop a long-term, holistic frame of reference. For example, the staff of a professional association, concerned about public opinion toward the industry they represented, constructed a futures wheel to explore the possible effects of a public education effort they were considering. At the center of a sheet of paper that covered an office wall they wrote, "New Public Relations Venture." They then drew lines from that to circles in which they wrote the possible social, economic, political, and technological consequences of the venture. As weeks passed, staff members and visitors added more circles filled with additional potential consequences. Soon they were connecting circles, showing how some consequences could have an impact on others. The association staff discussed which consequences were preferable and which were not. They developed a better understanding of what their

A PORTION OF THEIR FUTURES WHEEL

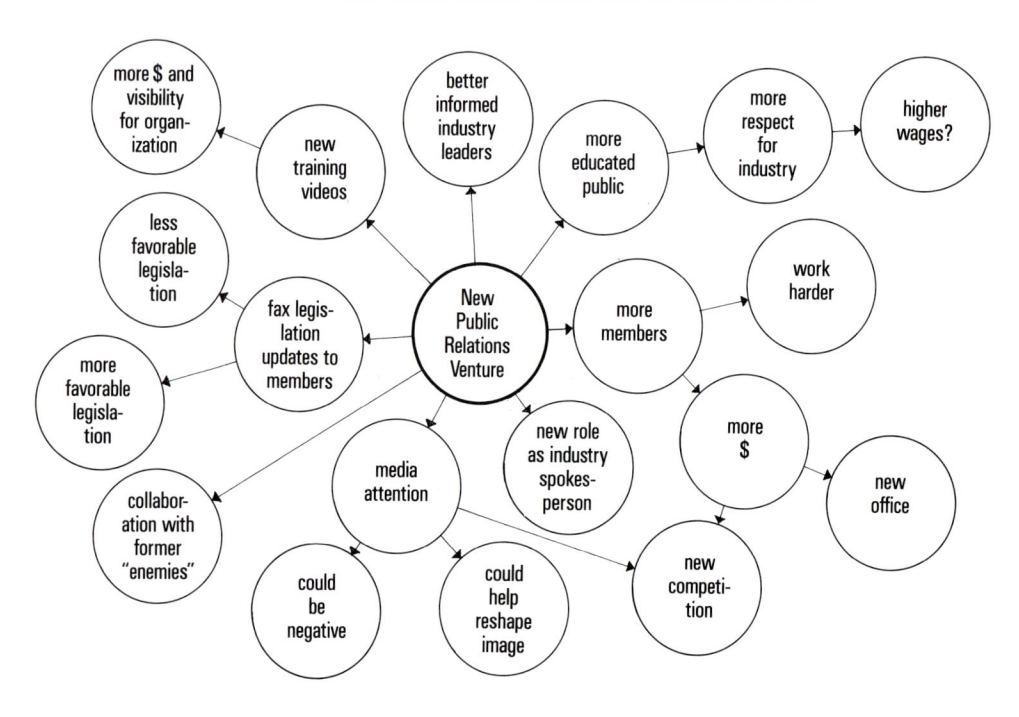

proposed venture might produce and what its most likely opportunities and pitfalls were. In addition, they gained important information on how to structure the venture for optimal success. An unexpected benefit was the buy-in for the project that developed on the part of all who had participated in its examination.

A long-term, global perspective will be so important in the future that parents and teachers should help every child develop this ability. With guidance, children can develop a global, long-term perspective in the course of their regular activities. When we read stories to children about people in different countries or environments, we can ask them to imagine what the characters in those stories would like and dislike if they came to visit. When we read about children in our own culture, we can ask young listeners to imagine what these children might be like as grown-ups.

Adults who want to further develop their long-term, global perspectives can practice by asking the following kinds of questions when they face a decision:

- What are the possible, probable, and preferable short-term consequences?
- What are the possible long-term consequences?
- What are the probable long-term consequences?
- What are the positive and negative aspects of these long-term consequences?
- What outcomes and consequences do I really want? Which can I live with?
- What can be done to reduce the negative impact of consequences or choices?
- What is likely to be the impact on others?
- Are there environmental considerations that need to be identified?
- What are the interests of others who may not have a powerful voice?

We can also strengthen our long-term, global perspective by trying to see the connections among seemingly unrelated events and factors. When we start to search for these connections, they begin to reveal themselves to us, almost magically. We start to see how changes our employers are introducing at work are connected to international trade, demographic shifts that affect the composition of the workforce, and a host of other issues. We discover that the long-term value of our personal assets is affected by a wide range of factors, some of which we have a measure of control over. We recognize, for example, patterns in the purchasing decisions of our clients or customers that we had never noticed before. By paying attention to linkages, we begin to think in a more anticipatory, systematic way — even about the most ordinary, day-to-day issues.

Organizations that want to encourage a long-term, global perspective in their employees can do so in a wide variety of ways. In the retail setting, a corporate headquarters might allow individual franchise stores more control over how they price and market products or provide them with training on how to reach local markets. Businesses might develop alternative courses of action based on potential market shifts and the introduction of new products. Organizations of all kinds could include a broader spectrum of employees in their strategic planning. Participative problem-solving sessions could address longer term, broader issues and connect them to immediate needs.

Building long-term, global thinking — and using it with the other traits described in this section — is a key component of effective function-driven leadership. When we become more anticipatory and systematic in our thinking, we can break free of the here-and-now demands that dominate our attention and determine our behavior.

CHAPTER ELEVEN

Concentrating on Quality

Virtually all outstanding leaders have one common characteristic: a compelling drive to excel, to be their best, to surpass their past performances. Whether they are artists, entrepreneurs, scientists, or athletes, individuals who concentrate on continually improving their performance stand out.

Similarly, organizations that focus on quality are easily distinguished from those that do not. They are dynamic, interactive companies where people work together toward common goals. They become learning organizations because their leaders are constantly setting goals, collecting and analyzing data, sharing feedback, and adjusting behaviors. They are able to improve performance by responding to changing external conditions. Members of learning organizations grow as individuals at the same time they are contributing to the growth of the organization.

Today's conditions require that people and organizations push beyond past accomplishments and seek higher and higher performance levels — even to attempt what they once may have considered impossible. The global marketplace, unprecedented economic conditions, social and demographic shifts, and increased competition all call for our very best efforts. We can no longer afford to settle for anything less.

This was not always so. For most of our lives, pyramid-shaped, bureaucratic organizations dominated the landscape.

Mediocrity was sufficient. In fact, those who strove for excellence at work or school were viewed with suspicion. Conformity was all we expected of workers and students, and those who tried to excel were often subjected to what Dr. Dee Henderson, director of the Federal Executive Institute in Charlottesville, Virginia, described to me as "crab management." Henderson explains:

> When I was in Micronesia, I learned about crab management. Government leaders there described their behavior as similar to crabs in a bucket. They said that it was unnecessary to put a lid on the bucket, because when one crab tried to climb out, the others pulled him back. Crab management is what develops when mediocrity is the norm; nobody wants anyone else to excel — we criticize, backbite, or do whatever we can to hold a climber down.

The results of our long acceptance of mediocrity can be witnessed in many arenas today. In education, students know they will not be held back in school if they fail to perform to certain standards. Unless they are aiming for one of a few prestigious schools, they know they can get into a college regardless of their grades. And they understand that the job market is such that their grades will probably be irrelevant in finding work. Parents who want their children to have higher standards can coach, coerce, threaten, or cajole all they want, but without any meaningful leverage their efforts are often in vain.

Too many adults, however, accept mediocrity for our young people just as they do in their own lives. In a recent study, mothers were asked what score they would be satisfied with on a math exam given to their child. The average score cited as acceptable by American mothers was 72, or a C; for Asian mothers it was 92, an A. Harold Stevenson, the University of Michigan professor who conducted the study, concluded, "Americans are satisfied with modest performance. It's not just in education; it transfers readily to industry. They're satisfied with 30 defects in 100,000 computer chips when the Japanese are not satisfied with one."

Stevenson is correct. Our standards in business and industry have been, to use his word, "modest." A pressure to conform to standards of mediocrity developed on assembly lines throughout the country, where workers who did their jobs too quickly were encouraged by their coworkers to slow down. This was a natural response, as management pressured workers to do more faster but not to engage their minds in the process. Modest standards seemed sufficient throughout the 1960s and 1970s. We still exported more goods than we imported. The rest of the world was hungry for American products, which were unlike anything they could purchase elsewhere.

Our modest standards have permeated every sector of society. Many government bureaucracies cling tenaciously to mediocrity. Ambitious, vocal, and conscientious employees are often labeled troublemakers or punished for being whistleblowers. Many managers who feel pressured to make changes dig in their heels. If they do make a move, they reorganize structures below them as if they were moving pawns in a chess game. Seldom do they dispense any real power or responsibility. They want others to do things differently, or even to do different things, but they want to maintain old patterns of behavior themselves.

In the public sector, such resistance has been tolerated for years. That will not be the case much longer. The National Performance Review recommendations for providing better government for less money emphasize customer service and quality. Even the U.S. Postal Service, for so long the target of ridicule and the very symbol of bureaucratic waste, has begun to restructure and redefine its mission. The Reinventing Government movement is shaking awake even the most comfortable federal agencies.

For many years W. Edwards Deming tried unsuccessfully to sound the alarm about the lack of commitment to quality in our country. In the late 1940s Deming suggested that improving quality would result in a competitive advantage for the American manufacturer. At the close of World War II, however, competition was not a major concern of U.S. manufacturers. Rebuffed year after year, Deming finally agreed in the 1950s to work with Japanese firms that were eager to adopt his ideas. The Japanese spent the next 40 years applying, refining, and expanding Deming's quality-improvement principles and beating the economic pants off the United States. Deming, who died in 1993 at the age of 92, always lamented the fact that his ideas became valuable to Americans only after the Japanese demonstrated their power.

In the early 1980s I had the opportunity to become the first Westerner to attend the annual quality awards banquet of Nippon Steel in Japan. As the teams that had offered the most important suggestions for improvement were honored, there were many quotes from and references to their "quality hero," Dr. Deming. After following Deming's principles for several decades, Japanese industry has turned the phrase "made in Japan" from a symbol of cheap, shoddy goods to one of quality that surpasses American standards. Beginning in the 1970s, Japanese companies (including those that produced automobiles, electronic appliances, and a host of other manufactured goods) emerged as global leaders, providing high-quality products at competitive prices.

David Kearns, a former undersecretary of education and corporate executive, reported returning from his twenty-fifth trip to Japan with a strong feeling about the key to Japanese success. He decided that the difference between the Japanese and American approaches to quality is that the Japanese have high expectations of themselves and Americans do not. On a plane trip to Japan, he had read a *Forbes* magazine article about a multibillion-dollar General Motors investment designed to make the company more competitive with the Japanese. The article's author, an American, concluded that GM would fail, and many at GM agreed with him. Their expectation of failure caused them to approach the investment half-heartedly. When Kearns arrived in Tokyo, he visited a Toyota plant, where he noticed copies of the *Forbes* article plastered all over the walls. He discovered that the Japanese auto workers assumed that GM would be successful and were already in the process of changing their standards, prices, and practices accordingly!

As economic conditions and business relationships have become more global, the Japanese have passed on their emphasis on continuous improvement to other nations. N.V. Philips, based in the Netherlands, is the world's largest producer of light bulbs. In the early 1980s, Nissan, a major customer, told Philips that not only would Philips have to reduce its defect rate from 500 per million to 100 per million, it would have to reduce its prices at the same time. Although assuming such a feat was impossible, Philips tried to meet these standards and, to its amazement, succeeded. Nissan then notified the company that it had to reduce the defect rate to 10 per million, then to 1 per million — and when Philips reached that goal, it was told it had to achieve a 1 in 10 million defect rate and reduce prices yet again. When Philips finally accomplished this seemingly miraculous feat, it credited Nissan with challenging the company to surpass standards it had previously considered impossible.

Americans generate millions of innovative ideas every year. But we have often failed to put our knowledge and creativity to work. In our personal, professional, and civic lives, there is great disparity between what we know how to do and what we actually deliver. Maybe we have lacked the will. Maybe we have not wanted excellence badly enough. Perhaps mediocrity has served us well enough that we have concluded that we could continue to put in as little effort as possible and not suffer any serious consequences. Whatever the reasons, innovative American ideas have been increasingly implemented for profit somewhere else in the world.

Only in the last few years, as the trade balance has dramatically turned against us (partially because the Japanese have so successfully adopted Deming's principles), has American business begun to heed the message about quality. Many leaders of American organizations are now quickly adjusting their business practices to try to improve quality. They have come to appreciate the simple axiom that organizations that produce higher quality products and services at lower costs than their competitors can expect to capture a greater share of the market.

Organizations with a focus on continuous improvement recognize that it is every employee's job to ensure quality. They are therefore investing in ways to strengthen employee skills, improve delivery systems, cut unnecessary cost and waste, and reward those who offer suggestions for improvement.

Some very promising steps are being taken in workplaces today to improve quality. In many cases, the approach involves giving employees more control over processes and products. Companies like Procter & Gamble are leading the way in developing self-managed work teams. H. James Harrington, president of the International Academy for Quality, says:

> Experience has shown that these self-managed work teams have had a major positive effect on both the quality of work life and the profitability of the organization in which this approach has been employed. Self-managed work teams improve productivity and quality, increase product ownership and pride, reduce cost and the need for overhead personnel, and boost employee morale.

Harrington tells of studying Globe Metallurgical, a producer of ferroalloys and silicon metal that was the first small company to win the Malcolm Baldrige National Quality Award. In three years, the organization increased productivity 380 percent and dramatically improved product quality and lowered cost by empowering employees to manage themselves. Other organizations have achieved similar results. Mr. Ralph Stayer, CEO of Johnsonville Sausage, reports that the turning point for his organization came the day he decided that he was no longer going to personally conduct the taste tests on the company's products. The employees, at first confused and alarmed, quickly reorganized themselves to manage quality control throughout the production process. He reports that they went on to create and implement many improvements that cut costs, improved quality, and ultimately increased sales and profits.

Decentralization seems to be a common theme among corporate leaders searching for quality. Anthony J. F. O'Reilly, chairman, president, and CEO of H.J. Heinz Company, reports that the benefits of decentralization include local and global advantages, increased speed and flexibility, and greater innovation. He reports:

In a decentralized enterprise like Heinz, the CEO and senior management must give affiliates a general sense of direction and a specific set of goals. Different CEOs have different styles for this. My style at Heinz is to exhort, to inspire, and to challenge our affiliates.... I am aided in this task by an incentive system that gives managers a direct stake in the outcome of the corporation.... Heinz's compensation system encourages realistic but aggressive goal-setting. It also attracts the kind of manager who is bolder and more ready to take risks.... All employees have been or are being trained in TQM methodology, myself included.

TQM is Total Quality Management, a process for ensuring continuous improvement by instituting specific quality-control measures. William W. McCarten, president of Host International, Inc., explains:

In today's volatile market, it's impossible not to change! Even as the leader in the market, we feel the need to change. Nobody can afford to become complacent or arrogant today. TQM plays an important role in helping manage change by providing a set of principles with specific techniques that can improve business. It is not a "feel good" mechanism.

Total Quality Management is getting plenty of attention in the public sector as well, and many local, state, and federal government units are using the system. The State of Wisconsin, for example, has had a TQM effort underway since 1989.

At the federal level, a Baldrige Award-like honor called the Quality Prototype Award is given to workplaces implementing TQM principles. One of the 1991 winners was the 1926th Communications-Computer Systems Group of the Air Force Logistics Command, which serves the information systems needs of 20,000 customers at Robbins Air Force Base in Georgia. In 1987, the 1926th embraced the Air Force's quality strategy called QP4 — quality people, quality process, quality performance, and quality product. In a summary of its efforts published by the Federal Quality Institute, the 1926th outlined the steps it took to achieve outstanding performance:

The first part is management, the transformation of functional managers into process managers and quality leaders. Second is methodology, the use of statistical process control and the other analytical techniques to improve our processes. Third is people, the transformation of the workforce into an empowered team performing at its full potential.... Through the use of this approach, results in productivity and quality of service have exceeded our expectations. For example, cost savings and avoidances have reached nearly $10 million over the past three years and, based on our feedback, customer satisfaction is at an all-time high.

As more public sector workplaces become interested in TQM, roadblocks to its success in that sector are being removed. In the past, government managers were given few in-

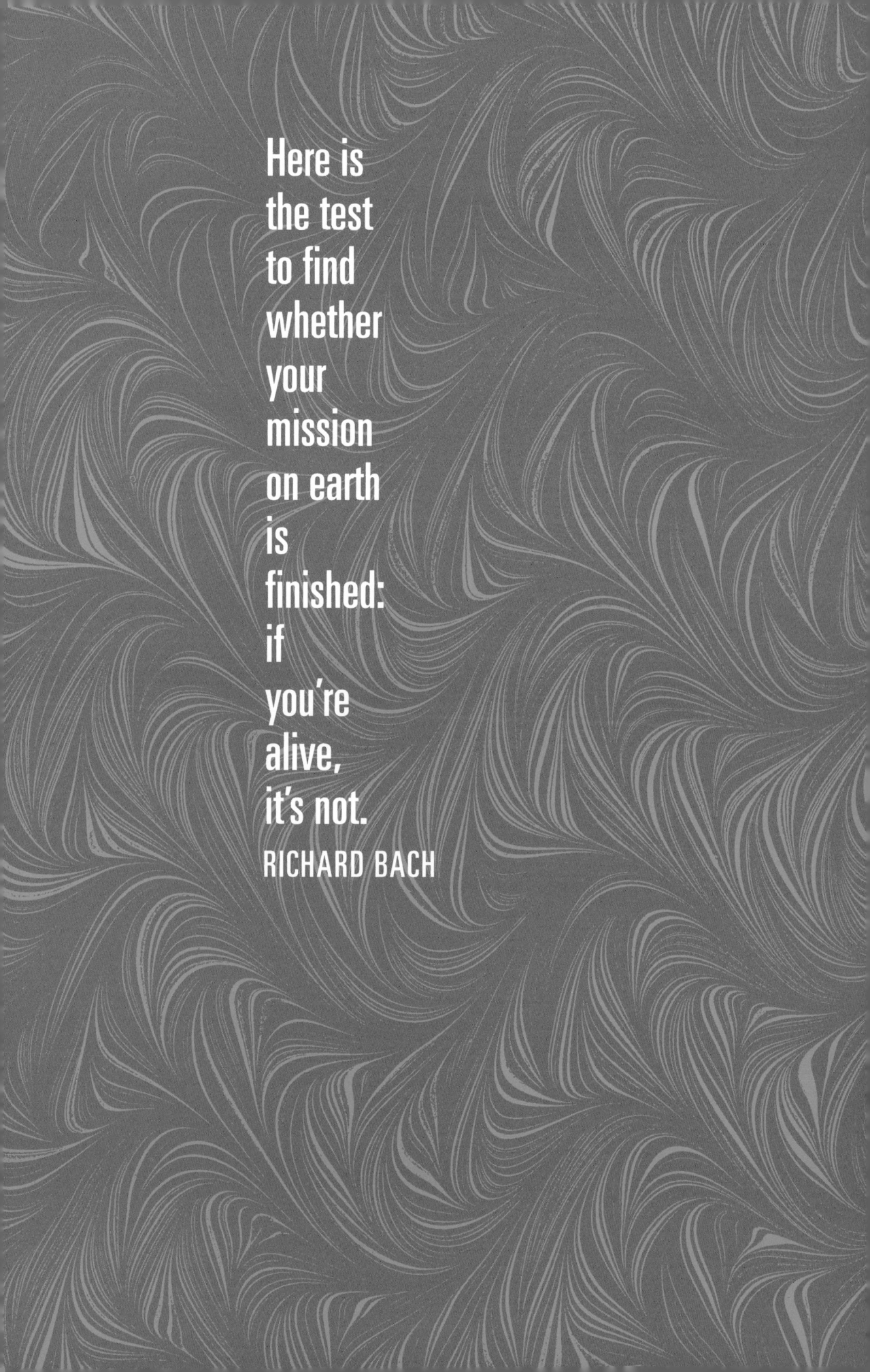

Here is
the test
to find
whether
your
mission
on earth
is
finished:
if
you're
alive,
it's not.
RICHARD BACH

centives and encountered many inhibitors when they tried to engage in TQM efforts. Among the most obvious problems was a disincentive to save money: when a federal agency shows a savings, the Office of Management and Budget (OMB) immediately takes the funds back. "If I tell OMB I've saved $168,000, I get $168,000 less next year — period," says a senior executive in a federal agency that has been practicing TQM since 1987. Since experts estimate that implementing TQM in the federal sector could save taxpayers $256 billion annually (about 20 percent of federal spending), the government has great reason to remove such impediments and actively encourage TQM.

Focus on quality is deeply interwoven with issues of values, norms, expectations, and power. Consequently, each organization develops its own unique style and pattern in its drive to achieve quality. Yet one characteristic correlates highly with success or failure of quality-improvement efforts: organizational leadership that is committed to change and willing to make fundamental changes itself. When leadership does not itself change, TQM becomes at best a charade and at worst exploitation of employees and other stakeholders.

Throughout the public sector, a debate is raging about the transferability from the private sector of TQM principles and practices. Ivan Kershner, principal of Colorado's Eagle Valley High School, is one educator who is not waiting for the experts to decide if TQM can be adapted to education. He and his staff are experimenting with TQM principles by initiating curriculum reform in which students must perform at an "A" level before they are allowed to advance. Kershner reasons that he and the staff have a responsibility to provide the learning environment, tools, and incentives to allow each student to perform "with zero defects." In a recent interview, Kershner told me,

This requires a complete paradigm shift in our thinking. References to
A-B-C-D-F permeate every aspect of our society. We have come to
expect some students to excel, some to be average, and some to fail.
Now, we can no longer think of a student's failure as his own; we need
to think of it as our collective failure and take responsibility for
correcting it. One thing we're discovering is that when students are clear
about what is expected of them and realize they will not advance unless
they perform at levels of excellence, they quickly demonstrate their
ability — in fact, willingness — to do so. There is no reason why, with
proper instruction, all students cannot get As.

In many ways, TQM is like religion. The basic tenets are useful guidelines for behavior, but when they become inflexible codes of conduct that are applied without common sense, they become ineffective, even damaging. Much suffering and pain has been inflicted in the name of religion; so too are

TQM efforts liable to cause problems if they are not part of a genuine commitment to function-driven values and practices. If an effort is labeled TQM but is used only to bolster pyramidal relationships and help those at the top squeeze more out of their employees, it is bound to fail. And it is not true TQM, which requires trust, open communication, and cooperation.

Individuals and organizations that want to improve performance can start by consulting books and articles or attending professional conferences that outline the characteristics of successful quality-improvement efforts. They can review their standards to ensure that they are high enough to be challenging but reasonable enough to encourage effort. They can establish benchmarks of success in attaining goals, either externally by examining the standards of the best in the field or internally by analyzing past performances, current resources, and future goals. Whichever path they choose, these individuals and organizations need to gather feedback from multiple sources on their progress, marking successes as well as failures.

It is important to monitor all the factors that influence quality, even those that may not appear at first to have a direct connection with performance. By paying attention to such factors, an individual may discover his personal performance is affected by how much sleep he has had, what he is wearing, how he feels about his colleagues, or how clearly he can imagine the performance he wants to give. A public figure may realize that her speeches are never quite as good if she makes them immediately following a press conference or interview. So she may decide to reschedule such events and conserve her energy. An executive may learn that he performs better at meetings when he knows those present. With this knowledge, he can decide to touch base earlier in the day with people who will be attending, and he can arrive at meetings early to introduce himself to newcomers, thus gaining comfort and confidence.

Organizations, likewise, can take many steps to improve quality. Staff members at one hotel, for example, were invited by management to a day-long retreat to discuss ways to improve the organization. Their discussion generated a host of insights and suggestions. One discovery was that when employees were late to work (which happened frequently), it triggered a chain of events that caused inefficiency and ineffectiveness. Staff members set a goal of zero-tardiness, analyzed and attacked the causes of tardiness, monitored their progress, made mid-course corrections, and by so doing improved their productivity tremendously. Employees set up a coffee room for those who came in early. They created a backup system so that those who ran into trouble with transportation, child care, or other causes of tardiness could call for help. Management provided the resources needed to implement these and other changes and encouraged employees to tackle additional problems. In the process, communications improved and team spirit grew. Employees began coming to work on time not because they were expected to by their bosses, but because their colleagues were counting on them and they recognized the chain reaction of negative events they would trigger if they were late.

We must keep in mind the interdependence of continuous improvement with the other function-driven leadership behaviors. As seen in many of the examples in this chapter, quality improvement and employee empowerment must go hand in hand.

A genuine emphasis on quality must also be linked to cooperation and collaboration. This leads to much higher levels of performance than when we adhere to our form-driven belief in competition, which results in policies and practices based on distrust. Successful athletes remind us that it is much more effective to try to surpass our own standards than to try to beat our competitors — especially if we view our own teammates as our competition.

CHAPTER TWELVE

Encouraging Innovation

In the past, our problems remained essentially the same from day to day, year to year, and generation to generation. The solutions of the past could be applied to the problems of the present with predictable results. But today's issues are radically different from those of the past. Identifying the causes of a problem is not as easy as it once was. Solutions that once worked increasingly fail. There is a dramatic need for fresh perspectives and innovative solutions. Yet we live in a society and work in organizations that often reinforce the low-risk, conformity-bound behaviors of the past.

As we enter the 21st century, the need for flexibility and innovation increases. Gordon F. Brunner, a Proctor & Gamble senior vice president, calls innovation "the marriage between what is needed and what is possible." C. Van der Klugt calls this characteristic "change-oriented." He says:

Change is the only constant that today's industry — indeed, society — can be certain of. To meet the changing scale and scope of work brought about by new technologies, many companies are changing their organizational structure, their products, and their market strategies. Future managers should be able to legitimize this change process, as well as create conditions for change by means of retraining programs for personnel. Most important, they too must be prepared for change by constantly renewing their information and learning new skills.

Innovation — creating new products, new services, new ways of turning out goods and services more efficiently — is becoming a most urgent concern of organizations everywhere. That is so, according to *Fortune* magazine, partly because restructuring has left many companies with a few core businesses that are solid but slow growing. *Fortune* concludes that, "innovation is their best bet for revving things up. In addition, technology has forced the pace of change and sharply cut the effective lifetimes of all kinds of products."

Many individuals and organizations are talking about being change-oriented, innovative, creative, and risk-taking, yet so many seem to have difficulty realizing these goals. This is often because they try to develop function-driven behaviors within the confines of form-driven institutions. Unless they also tackle the values and beliefs that support the pyramidal structure, their efforts will amount to little more than hopeful rhetoric.

To effect genuine, positive change, we need to understand the characteristics of innovative problem solving and how they differ from approaches of the past. The two styles of problem solving are outlined below.

Problem-Solving Styles

Form-Driven	Function-Driven
Avoids risks	Rewards calculated risk-taking
Values uniformity	Values creativity
Values blending in	Values challenging assumptions and going beyond conventional boundaries
Maintains bureaucracy	Fosters entrepreneurship
Does not accept failure	Expects some failure
Relies on the past	Focuses on the future as well as the past
Depends solely on what is "tried and true"	Experiments with new ideas and solutions
Emphasizes rules, structure	Emphasizes process, results
Accepts problems as previously defined	Redefines problems
Tinkers around the edges	Addresses core issues directly
Addresses symptoms	Attacks possible causes

Resistance to change and an inability to respond quickly and flexibly to new situations continue to hamper American families, businesses, and communities. In a recent survey of Fortune 500 executives, only half described recent efforts at change in their organizations as successful. Employee resistance to change was cited by 76 percent of respondents as the major factor that derailed their efforts. Clearly, one of the great challenges for future leadership is managing change and successfully helping others do the same.

Pyramidal organizations tend to reinforce form-driven problem solving. For a long time, the problems addressed by managers in such organizations varied little from year to year, thus requiring little innovation or creativity. Following established procedures and directions from one's superiors was appropriately valued more than generating new ideas. Likewise, many employers have not rewarded risk-taking. Employees often refuse to offer suggestions because they have come to believe that it is useless to do so — or worse, that they will actually get in trouble if they do. In Japan, each employee offers an average of 24 suggestions per year. In the United States, the average annual number of suggestions per employee is 0.14!

Today, we increasingly face problems unlike any we have tackled in the past. Even the most stable pyramidal organizations — like IBM, Sears, American Express, and General Motors — are experiencing complex new problems that time-honored practices cannot solve. Their survival depends on their leaders learning function-driven problem-solving techniques. Yet these individuals became leaders in the first place by working their way to the top of pyramidal organizations, which rewarded form-driven thinking. All too often, senior executives have demonstrated a method of problem solving that has become inappropriate for many contemporary issues. They have been so richly rewarded for these abilities that it is hard for them to imagine or appreciate any other approach. Although they are often intelligent and motivated individuals who *want* to be successful leaders, they are limited by their experience.

In spite of this, many organizations are trying hard to change their corporate cultures to encourage and reward function-driven, innovative behaviors. Johnson & Johnson urges change and risk-taking. Its chief, James Burke, says, "We want change here. I try to give people the feeling that it's okay to fail, that it's important to fail." Other organizations encourage innovation through financial incentives. Monsanto, for instance, annually offers a $50,000 prize to the scientist or team of scientists that develops commercially successful products.

Some organizations are changing their old cultures by setting up interdepartmental teams and task forces that allow members to try out new behaviors not permitted in the old pyramidal structure. These groups are encouraged to be entrepreneurial and operate outside of old corporate norms. Risk-taking and innovation are rewarded, and failure is considered part of the learning process. Effective leaders make it known that these groups are charting a course that the rest of the organization will soon follow. When these efforts are most successful, it is because top management changes its own behavior to model want they want from their employees.

Like organizations in the private sector, public sector organizations need to emphasize innovation and creative problem-solving, especially as they experience increased competition from the private sector. This is difficult for many to do. Rondeau Gurley, former director of the Human Resources Development Division of the U. S. Department of Agriculture, explains:

Innovation and risk-taking are still not rewarded in the federal government. The system prohibits real risk-taking. We are rewarded for looking good and trying hard, rarely for achievement or accomplishment. The status quo reigns with a vengeance. This has to change. There has to be an award and reward system that acknowledges achievement and risk-taking. There is no such system now. Our performance evaluation system needs to focus on achievement of goals and de-emphasize how pleasant someone looks, how compliant they are, and how hard they appear to try.

A few government leaders are beginning to encourage work units to set their own objectives to support the agency's mission and to chart a course for achieving them. Traditional evaluation methods, where supervisors use subjective techniques to rate individual employees, often focusing on their deficiencies, are giving way to more innovative techniques. Frequently, teams are evaluated collectively, and team members participate in the process. Employees are being rated more by the quality of the products or services their teams produce than by managers' perceptions of their personalities. One new tool being used in the federal government is called a "360." Employees are rated by those above, below, and at their level, giving them a 360-degree view of their colleagues' perceptions of their strengths and weaknesses.

In the public sector, even more so than in the private sector, mid-level management often needs special help in making the transition to such function-driven leadership behaviors as innovation and risk-taking. Mid-level managers frequently — and understandably — fear losing power, promotions, or even their jobs. They often do not know what is expected of them or what they have to gain by altering old patterns of behavior. They need extra attention to ensure that whatever changes are being proposed are more attractive to them than the status quo.

I recently attended an international meeting of futurists where a keynote speaker, a change consultant to hospitals, addressed the issue of employee resistance to change. She told of a hospital that had hired her to persuade its nurses to adopt new technologies. She proudly recounted the techniques she used to force them into acquiescence. Part way through her story she revealed that the new technologies were designed to eventually replace nurses. No wonder the nurses were reluctant! Viable change cannot be accomplished through hidden agendas or dishonest approaches. Nor can it be at the expense of those expected to adopt it. In efforts to introduce innovations, as in every other human transaction, honesty about motives and expected outcomes is essential.

Another trap to avoid is encouraging employees to be innovative and creative when the organization is not ready to reinforce their efforts. Few approaches are more damaging to an organization and its employees than urging people to take risks, only to revert back to old values and punish employees if their efforts at innovation fail, go too far, or violate established norms. This happens too often, causing people to become even more risk-averse.

Like all function-driven leadership traits, an orientation toward change and innovation cannot succeed in isolation. It must be developed in conjunction with other function-driven leadership skills. For instance, efforts to innovate depend on open communications and cooperation. Nothing can hamper innovation more than a lack of coordination among the various parts of an organization. SmithKline Beecham, a champion at introducing new products, learned this painful lesson when its researchers developed a vaccine for hepatitis. Company researchers made this scientific breakthrough in the early 1980s, but company marketers rejected it because SmithKline Beecham did not normally sell vaccines in the United States. After repeated unsuccessful attempts to persuade the marketers to reconsider, the researchers finally convinced the international division to try the product, which met with immediate success. "Too bad they did not listen to us a couple of years ago," says a SmithKline research vice president. "They would have a $100 million drug by now."

Once we recognize the need to take fresh approaches to problems, how can we learn to do so? Fortunately, there are many ways to improve this ability. One is to "break set," which means to push past the walls of the pyramid. Breaking set opens up our thinking process, allowing us to view problems, situations, and experiences in original ways and from different perspectives.

We forfeit three-fourths of ourselves to be like other people.
ARTHUR SCHOPENHAUER

I miss 100% of the shots I don't take.
WAYNE GRETSKY

Results! Why, man I have gotten a lot of results. I know several hundred that would not work.
THOMAS EDISON

There are many techniques that help us break set and look at issues in new ways. Playfulness and laughter are helpful: "ha-ha's" often lead to "ah-ha's." Interacting with new people and new ideas makes breaking set easier, as does a relaxed or fresh environment. A nonjudgmental atmosphere also encourages us to explore new ways of thinking; there is always plenty of time later to critique the ideas we generate. Some problem solvers break set by tackling a problem from as many different angles as possible. This helps them get out of their pyramidal thinking and look at a problem from new perspectives.

Another key to improving flexibility and creativity is to practice generating as many ideas, solutions, and alternatives as possible. The more ideas we have, the more likely we are to have good innovative ones. Two-time Nobel Prize-winner Linus Pauling said, "The best way to get a good idea is to get a lot of ideas." Emile Chartier, French philosopher and teacher, put it this way: "Nothing is more dangerous than an idea when it is the only one you have."

The first batch of ideas we generate about an issue is often form-driven, reflecting common, pyramid-bound thinking. The more we know about a subject, the more adaptive ideas we will have about it. But if we push beyond our form-driven ideas, another set of ideas starts to flow, different from the first and often more innovative, creative, and function-driven.

As an experiment, try generating a list of names of birds. The more of an expert you are, the longer you will be able to remain in a form-driven mode and draw on your recall skills. Regardless of the length of your list, eventually you will run out of names. You can quit — or you can generate innovative ones. You might think of Larry Bird, Charlie Byrd, Lady Bird Johnson, Tweetie Bird, Stravinsky's Firebird, Road Runner, the Baltimore Orioles, Big Bird, *Bye Bye Birdie*, and so on. As you become more innovative, you will notice an energy shift. You will be using additional brain power, having more fun, and blazing new trails. Although some of the ideas you generate may seem silly, this technique — brainstorming — often leads to important breakthroughs.

Brainstorming is a well-known method of generating ideas, but there are many others, including brainwriting (ideas are written on pieces of paper, exchanged among group members, and built on), brainboarding (an adaptation of story-boarding, ideas are placed on cards and then arranged on a large board), and the use of trigger concepts (a series of words or pictures are used to "trigger" fresh perspectives on an issue). All idea-generation techniques operate under the same ground rules.

We can all exercise our ability to be more flexible, creative, innovative, and risk-taking in our everyday lives. We can

> **Ground Rules for Idea Generation**
>
> - Produce as many ideas as possible — go for quantity.
>
> - Piggyback — build on others' ideas.
>
> - Stretch for "far-out" ideas — the wilder the better.
>
> - Hold criticism. Don't utter killer phrases, such as, "We've already tried that," "The boss would never let us do it," "We could never afford that," or make killer looks and gestures, such as folding your arms and rolling your eyes.

search for as many different ways as possible to do our morning routine. We can find new meals to cook — and new ways to prepare our old favorites. We can find alternative routes to some of our frequent destinations. We can explore new reading material. We can experiment with different styles of clothing. We can search for fresh solutions to household problems. We can reorganize our living or work space. We can initiate a new hobby or exercise program. Becoming comfortable with changes that we can control at the personal level limbers us up for the larger scale, higher risk changes that await us in the world.

CHAPTER THIRTEEN

Improving Cooperation and Communication

An executive who hires and manages hundreds of high-level researchers recently told me, "There are more Ph.D.s today who are unemployed because they cannot communicate and be team players than for any other reason." I think his observation was a suitable epitaph for the days when highly successful people could work in isolation. Today, people and organizations that can communicate and cooperate are those most likely to succeed. In fact, the proliferation of unexpected partnerships may be one of the most visible signs of how dramatically the world is changing. The saying, "One step by 100 persons goes farther than 100 steps by one person," is a prescription for progress.

The need for improved communication and cooperation was voiced by virtually every leader interviewed for this book. And efforts at improving cooperation and communication can be seen in every arena. On the international scene, we are witnessing new political, economic, and social collaborations that just a few years ago would have seemed impossible.

In 1990 Lee Iacocca announced that Chrysler was going to take on the Japanese in a new corporate advertising campaign. The campaign touted the Chrysler "advantage" and featured pointed comparisons between American and Japanese products. Iacocca himself appeared in the ads, engaging in the increasingly popular practice of "Japan bashing." Yet just one year later *The Economist* reported, "With his company running on empty and the American government unwilling to bail it out for a second time, there is only one place left for Chrysler's Japan-bashing chairman, Lee Iacocca, to turn: Japan." Chrysler's subsequent collaboration with Mitsubishi, called Diamond Star Motors (DSM), was initially hailed as a "bold new partnership," an equal collaboration between the Japanese and American automakers.

Actually, the agreement with DSM was the most recent expansion of a 20-year relationship that allowed both companies to better compete in the global marketplace. In describing the relationship, DSM president and CEO Yoichi Nakane said, "Working together, we have built a very productive and efficient plant. We have each accepted responsibility for our own jobs while at the same time cooperating with each other. Since our groundbreaking, Diamond Star Motors has enjoyed what we Japanese call *Wa* — harmony among people."

Iacocca publicly embraced the contentious, competitive leadership characteristics of the pyramid when he thought they would be economically beneficial, but privately he behaved more collaboratively when forced to do so by economic necessity. Although Iacocca made this kind of straddling an art form, many of today's leaders who try to operate simultaneously out of opposing paradigms are unsuccessul. What makes Iacocca unusual is that publicly he appeared to be form-driven while privately he was more function-driven. Most leaders who straddle the two paradigms do the opposite. They profess to be function-driven but behave in old form-driven patterns.

In July 1991, arch computer rivals IBM and Apple announced an alliance. Industry analyst Charles R. Wolf of First Boston Corporation said, "I do not think anything stranger has happened." Only a day before the IBM-Apple deal, IBM announced another big venture with the German electronics company Siemens to develop a new generation of memory chips. *Newsweek* reported, "For the world's largest computer maker, the deals were an acknowledgment that tough times require change; for the first time, IBM is turning to outsiders for help."

That same year, Apple struck an accord with Toshiba Corporation of Japan to develop systems for both firms' computer equipment. This was the first formal relationship Apple had made with a Japanese computer maker, although it had previously purchased parts from Japan. Apple's continuing strategy is to build relationships with the Japanese instead of trying to outdo them. The company recently refused to join a consortium of U.S. semiconductor and computer manufacturers organized as a competitive response to foreign manufacturing of D-RAM chips. The consortium soon fell apart.

Cross-national alliances are taking place in virtually every industry: General Electric and Ishikawajima-Harima Heavy Industries are working together to build a new line of jet engines; BellSouth has joined forces with Sony to test a wireless telephone system in Georgia; Kobe Steel and Aluminum Company of America have formed an alliance to produce aluminum beverage cans.

In education, the National Education Association and the American Federation of Teachers, two long-time bitter rivals, are cooperating on several joint ventures, and have begun merger discussions. Such a merger would bring all U.S. teachers into one union, an idea that just a few years ago was unthinkable. The two international organizations with which the NEA and AFT are affiliated have already merged.

This recent surge in partnerships is also bringing together leaders in totally different sectors of society — often for the first time. As leaders recognize the artificial boundaries of the form-driven paradigm, they look for new ways to meet increasingly complex and interconnected problems with fewer resources. For example, in the last decade, many successful business/education/government partnerships have been formed to improve the quality of American education and provide American industry with a better-prepared workforce. As it is, U.S. businesses are currently spending about $210 billion annually on formal and informal employee training — about two-thirds of the country's total annual expenditure on its public schools.

Although these partnerships between business, education, and the government come in many shapes and sizes, they all bring private-sector perspectives and resources to the effort to address the increasing demands placed on education. According to the organizers of the Building Excellent Schools Through Business-Education Teamwork (BEST-BET) project in Burlington, Massachusetts, the results include "lower drop-out rates; improved student achievement; a higher quality, happier, and more stable teaching community; improved school administration; a better understanding of education by the outside community; and fully functioning, well-maintained school facilities and equipment." The businesses involved report improved public relations, morale, and outlook, all an outgrowth of knowing that they are helping build the kind of high-quality workforce that is essential to the country's future.

Private-public partnerships have always existed, but in the past they were exceptions to the rule. Now they are the rule. Many private-public partnerships are launched in one community and spread to others. One creative example of what can be accomplished through private-public partnerships is the School Care Fair, of Tucson, Arizona. Recently, staff and volunteers at the local food bank became frustrated that all they could give families was food when they needed so much more. So they invented a School Care Fair, to be held at a neighborhood school at the end of summer. Its goal was to prepare low-income children for school and, in the process, improve coordination among child-service agencies. All participating agencies had to agree to provide a free service at the site and have an agency decision maker attend all of the planning meetings.

Twenty-six agencies gathered for the Care Fair, where children had their vision checked, their transfers to new schools processed, and their blood tested for sickle-cell anemia. They received Social Security numbers, immunizations, and physicals. Representatives from Head Start and other programs were there to sign up eligible families. Parents could register to vote, learn about a nonprofit clothing bank, get bus passes for their children, and receive help in finding daycare for their preschoolers. Not only were the services needed and appreciated; everyone had a good time.

Perhaps the greatest long-term benefit was that the participating agencies learned more about one another and improved their communication and cooperation. Clients reported fewer instances of being sent needlessly from agency to agency, and referrals made more sense. The next year, the program was expanded to two sites for the two weekends before the start of school. For about $4,000 in advertising and custodial expenses, 1,400 families with roughly 4,000 children were provided the support to successfully launch the school year.

Cooperation and communication are just as important within organizations as among them. One key to successful communication within an organization is the ability and willingness to listen. When William Crouse took over ODSI, a subsidiary of Johnson & Johnson, the first thing he did was nothing — except wander through the halls of the organization, stopping in every office, seeking ideas, asking questions, and listening. He knew that to change the existing top-down organizational style to a more collaborative strategy-setting model he had to encourage people to communicate their fears, frustrations, hopes, and dreams. Crouse spent his second three months talking with virtually every employee. He recalls, "I then reported back to them saying, 'This is what you've told me about the company, and here are my conclusions based on what you've told me. This is what I think we should do; now, what do you think?'" This clear and deliberate effort to really listen to employees and then build on what they said was the beginning of a remarkable improvement in productivity and employee satisfaction.

In government, education, and industry, labor and management were once pitted against each other in traditional competitive relations. Now both sides frequently share information and, together, seek solutions to mutual problems. Win-win negotiations are replacing the traditional win-lose approach of the past. Teams composed of both management and labor are working to overcome bureaucratic hurdles and tackling such tough issues as health care expenses.

Predictably, many heads of organizations are initially resistant to the degree of open communication and cooperation such efforts require. Helping the heads of organizations acknowledge and overcome their fear of losing control and trust the consensus-building process is one of the greatest challenges I face as a consultant. Yet, in every case in which those at the top have opened up communication and encouraged cooperation, they were pleasantly surprised and richly rewarded by the results. Without fail, stakeholders who were included in decision making acted responsibly and made valuable contributions. Certainly, using a professional facilitator can smooth out the process, but most organizations can expect positive results by simply making more information available to more people.

In education, competition and one-way communication were mainstays of the schools most of us attended. But how will young people learn to communicate and cooperate in the future if schools cling to these behaviors of the past? Fortunately, many schools are changing. Cooperative and collaborative learning have become popular teaching strategies. Students no longer sit silently in their seats, neatly arranged in rows, listening to the teacher. They work in groups, sharing their opinions and trying to reach consensus on problems. A sign I saw in one classroom where cooperative learning was taking place summed up this view:

> **None of us is more able than all of us.**

With a function-driven paradigm, collaboration replaces competition as the cornerstone of productive behavior. Open communication and mutual trust replace secrecy and self-promotion. Although some of this cooperation is occurring for altruistic motives, much of it is initially bred of economic necessity. Sharing precious resources and information for mutual benefit is becoming the norm because we can no longer afford wasteful and misplaced competition.

Leaders who want to improve their communication and collaboration skills can find countless resources to support their efforts. Many books and seminars discuss new styles of negotiation, communication in multicultural environments, male-female communication styles, team building, business alliance formation, and collaborative problem solving. Those who want to strengthen their abilities to communicate and cooperate should work on their listening and observation skills, find new partners for joint ventures, coach others who need support, and request feedback from those around them.

On every level, cooperation and communication are vitally important. We need these skills to manage our interpersonal relationships and our daily lives. Our personal and professional success depends on them. For organizations, improving cooperation and communication can lead to increased productivity, greater employee satisfaction, and higher quality of products and services. It is this simple: Cooperation is possible only with trust and open communication. Without cooperation, nothing important can be achieved.

CHAPTER FOURTEEN

Committing to Ethical Practices

The rigid structure of the pyramid system suited social and ethical mores for most of this century. For many years, there was little confusion about the nature of the world, what was right or wrong, or the rules of the game. In retrospect, the 1950s seem like a Norman Rockwell painting — and the embodiment of pyramid values. Life then was much more predictable and categorical. Men were either blue-collar workers, white-collar workers, or farmers. Generally, they worked their entire career in the organization in which they started. My grandfather, an immigrant to this country, proudly retired after 50 years at the Ford Motor Company. He worked in only one plant in 50 years — a plant that does not even exist today. He, and many like him, married, bought a home, raised a family, took vacations, and retired with a gold watch without ever thinking that he might be laid off, that his plant might be closed with little or no warning, or that his retirement benefits might not be there when he needed them.

In that stable, homogeneous society, most Americans shared a common value system and agreed on what was right and wrong. Democracy and capitalism were considered good, communism and dictatorships bad. Being, or striving to be, middle class was good, and upper middle class was even better. The nuclear family, which consisted of a father who worked, a mother who stayed home, some children, and a pet or two, was good.

Television cooperated in painting this simple landscape by providing us with shows like *Our Miss Brooks, Father Knows Best,* and *Ozzie and Harriet.* Fashion was dictated by the designers, and styles were clearly either "in" or "out." For most Americans — and in fact, most of the "free world" — the United States was demonstrably the greatest country on earth, the world leader economically, politically, militarily, and culturally. We were proud to be Americans and had no confusion about our country's role in the world.

How different it is today, when many of us feel like unwilling passengers on a runaway train, being thrust forward, hurled from side to side, and then slammed back. We feel out of control and careening toward an uncertain fate. Few of the old rules apply either at home or abroad. The transitory nature of our lives — and our values — can be seen everywhere.

Not long ago, as I drove into a rest stop in Michigan, just over the Ohio border, I saw a driver take an Ohio State University baseball cap off the back window ledge of his car and replace it with a University of Michigan cap. Our loyalties and commitments seem to shift just as easily. We have all been handed business cards with a company name on them but with a space left for members of an ever-changing workforce to insert their names. What a far cry this is from the days when both employer and employee expected each other to be around — and together — for 50 years!

Beginning in the 1960s and more visibly in the 1970s, as form-driven institutions began to show visible signs of decay, traditional values also began to crumble. Mass communication revealed the inequities in our society. People became aware that life for many Native Americans, African Americans, recent immigrants, and others was not a Norman Rockwell painting. Those for whom the pyramid did not work could see how richly others were rewarded and how unfairly they were being treated. Distinctions between right and wrong became increasingly blurred. Behaviors once considered safe, clear, and accepted were routinely challenged. There was no longer a clear consensus of who the good guys and bad guys were, internationally or interpersonally.

In the early 1970s, there was an open backlash against the values of form-driven institutions. The Vietnam War brought the clash to the forefront of our national agenda. People started to view values as more relative than absolute — or their values as absolutely correct and others' as absolutely wrong. An illustration of the shift toward relativism is the values clarification movement that swept education in the early 1970s. According to *Values Clarification: A Handbook of Practical Strategies for Teachers and Students,* published in 1972 and authored by Sidney B. Simon, Leland W. Howe, and Howard Kirschenbaum, the concern was "not...with the *content* of people's values, but the *process of valuing.*" They believed that the way you arrived at your values was important, not what those values were. Imagine, for example, the confusion this point of view stirred in young, idealistic teachers when values clarification trainers insisted that the appropriate teacher response to a student who had just shouted a racial slur was a clarifying question such as, "John, how do you *feel* about having made that statement to Martin?"

In the late 1970s and throughout the 1980s, consensus on form-driven values eroded further. The values of the function-driven paradigm had not yet sufficiently emerged, thus creating a values void. During this time, many individuals and institutions avoided public discussions not only of pyramidal values, which were increasingly problematic, but of all values whatsoever. Because any attention to values seemed likely to provoke someone, many chose to project an image of being objective and "value-free."

Leaders in government, business, religion, education, and other arenas grabbed on to this life raft of objectivity. Standardized, "objective" evaluation methods became even more popular in assessing employee productivity, quality of service, environmental safety, student progress, teacher competence, crime reduction, and every other important aspect of society. In each case, the assessment was claimed to be accurate, complete, and, above all, objective.

In truth, such objective measures were far from value-free. What they measured depended on having data that was easy to analyze. The data, however, were easily manipulated and provided results that were often biased, contradictory, or even inaccurate. Most often, they painted a woefully inadequate picture of the scene they purported to capture.

This determination to be viewed as objective allowed managers in pyramid-bound institutions to abdicate personal responsibility for their actions. They hired and fired based not on what they thought or felt but on what they considered to be "objective criteria." They would close factories, send troops into foreign lands, fail students, and pollute the environment with clear consciences, convinced that these were not personal decisions but were required by the conditions and criteria established by others.

Because teachers had come under fire in the 1970s for teaching values in their classrooms, many principals and school boards rooted out all value-oriented materials and activities from the curriculum. Some conservative groups monitored school textbook companies, protesting ideas they found objectionable. Consequently, many publishers capitulated and expunged anything remotely resembling controversial themes, words, or values from their books. Many teachers of that time remember their bewilderment at receiving new editions of textbooks that deleted the most engaging readings and activities of previous editions. Textbook publishers wanted to be safe rather than sorry; they had removed *anything* that *anyone* might object to so that they could sell the same textbook throughout the United States, including in regions where the textbook censors had the most influence. Among educators, this is often called the "dumbing-down" of the curriculum.

In many work, school, and community environments, it became socially unacceptable and politically incorrect to address values directly. Into the void created by the decline of traditional values crept a rise in traditional vices: greed, corruption, and "me-first" attitudes. A "get-what-you-can-while-the-gettin's-good" mentality emerged. Many of those exploiting the system voiced their strong commitment to traditional values while they systematically took all they could get from their investors, voters, parishioners, or employees. And nobody stopped them. The government, boards of directors, the public, and others to whom these individuals should have been accountable simply stood by.

Previous eras certainly had their rogues and rascals, from the robber barons to the Watergate collaborators, but during the 1980s greed seemed to become socially acceptable. One social commentator recently called it the decade of the ethically challenged. An American Hall of Infamy for the 1980s would include Jimmy Swaggart, Ivan Boesky, Charles Keating, Leona Helmsley, Marion Barry, the crew at Saloman Brothers, BCCI, the crooks in the Savings and Loan scandals, and a host of corporate heads who have admitted to lying on safety inspections, bribing government contractors, and cheating their stockholders and the government out of billions of dollars. And let us not forget evangelical leader Jim Bakker, who captured the spirit of the decade when he declared, "Christ died for our sins. Dare we make his martyrdom meaningless by not committing them?"

Organizations as well as individuals operated in a values void. If they did nothing illegal, they still, in the spirit of objectivity, looked the other way. Stanford University, a bastion of academic excellence, was rocked by revelations of excessive research charges billed to taxpayers. Its president resigned; he had difficulty explaining to federal auditors $200 million in improper expenses, including a cedar-lined closet in his residence, use of a 72-foot yacht, and administrative costs for a shopping

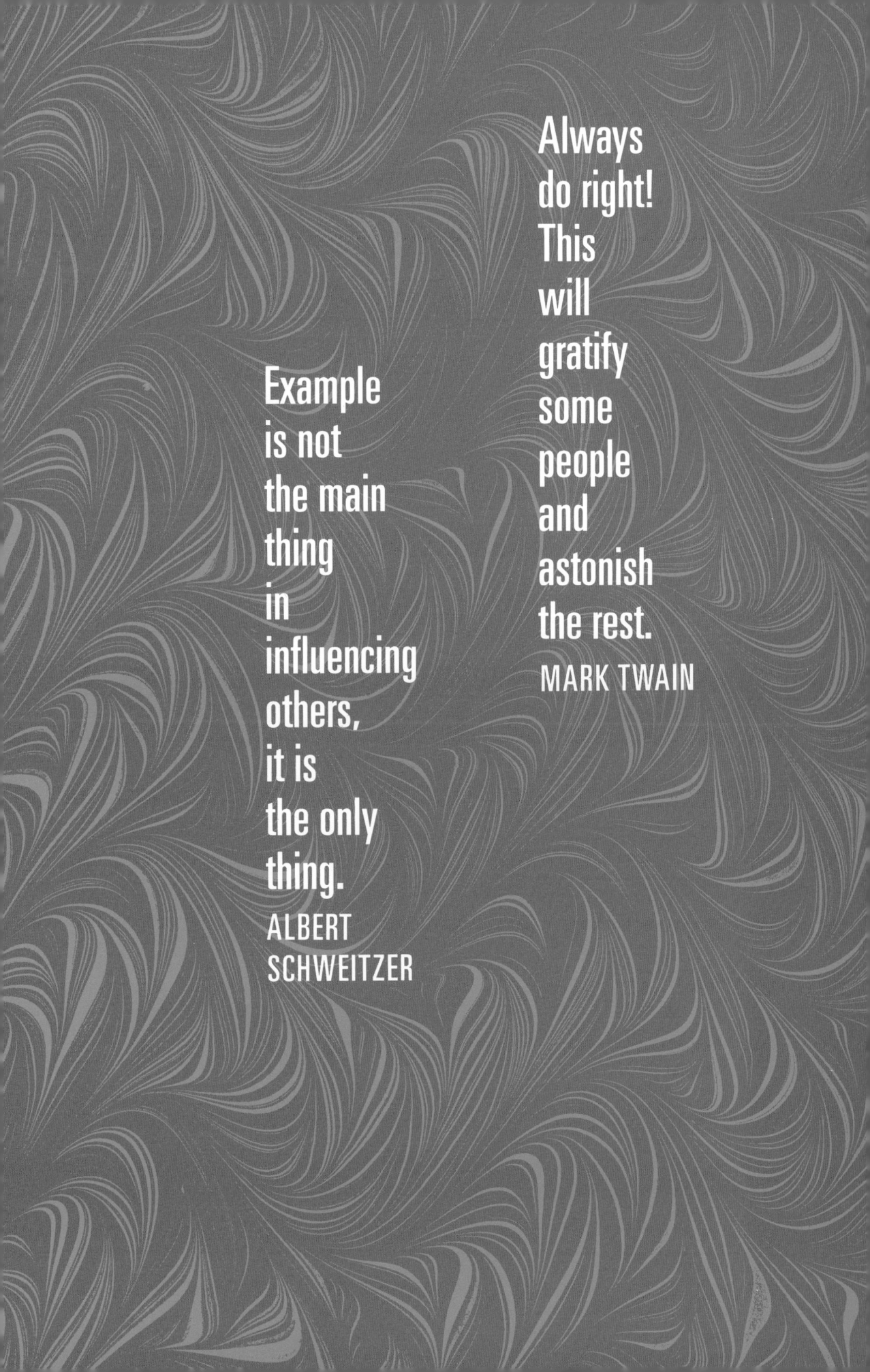

Example is not the main thing in influencing others, it is the only thing.
ALBERT SCHWEITZER

Always do right! This will gratify some people and astonish the rest.
MARK TWAIN

center on university property. United Way of America was rocked by scandals surrounding the behavior of its president, whose excesses became headline news.

There is less and less tolerance for such abuse today. We are witnessing a shift away from the "me-ism" created by the values void of the last two decades. A greater concern with ethics is emerging. The old form-driven values are receding or being redefined.

Whether we recognize it yet or not, a new set of ethics is emerging. Its characteristics include a growing consensus that our mutual interests outweigh our differences, a respect for diversity while we build on shared goals, behavior based on what is right, not just what is expedient or profitable, and consideration of the long-term consequences of actions and the effects those actions will have on others, including those with less power.

A function-driven ethic offers a framework for balancing individual and collective interests so that people and organizations have both freedom and responsibility. It is neither moralistic, like the pyramid model, nor completely relativistic. It values different points of view in the context of widely agreed-on principles of behavior. So we might agree that we can disagree on an issue but will limit the expression of our disagreements to acceptable avenues — choosing peaceful, legal means to advance our position rather than violence and illegal actions.

This global ethic is inclusive rather than exclusive. It casts a circle that seeks to draw in all people and groups rather than leaving some out. The major proponents of this emerging global ethic are not only those at the top of the pyramid. They are often people who have been at the bottom or middle — ordinary people who reject the profit-driven, either/or, black-and-white values of the past for a more inclusive, purpose-oriented model.

A recent event I attended illustrated what the emerging global ethic is all about. Sponsored by Independent Sector, a nonprofit organization that promotes the interests of the voluntary sector, the event was held to welcome Independent Sector's new chairperson, Raul Yzaguirre, president of the National Council of La Raza. I noticed that participants included corporate CEOs along with representatives of refugee groups and gay and lesbian coalitions, AIDS activists, environmental lawyers, and volunteer accountants. The event was held at the Sasakawa Peace Foundation USA, a Japanese philanthropic organization based in Washington, D.C., and sponsored by the National Trust for Historic Preservation, the Fannie Mae Foundation, and Matsushita Electric Corporation of America. Now that is what I call transcending traditional boundaries to work together toward common goals!

The transition to this new function-driven ethic is being supported by different elements in society working together. For example, the federal government is providing incentives to help corporations focus on ethics. Andrew W. Singer, editor of *Ethikos,* a publication that examines ethical standards in business, identifies one of the most important events in the area of corporate ethics. He notes the recent change in government guidelines for penalizing corporations that have broken the law by violating ethics standards. According to Singer, the government is now making a distinction between corporations that have effective compliance programs and those that do not. It offers a seven-step set of instructions for setting up compliance programs, including ethics training, hotlines for whistle-blowers, and other mechanisms to encourage ethical behavior. If the government recognizes that a corporation has a generally effective compliance program, fines for violations are reduced according to a fixed formula. For many corporations this is a strong incentive to focus on ethics. Concluded Singer in a recent interview, "It's great to see the government using the carrot as well as the stick in motivating corporations to act ethically."

As Secretary of Labor Robert Reich is fond of pointing out, for the first time in our nation's history, much of what is economically rewarding is also socially beneficial. Self-interest and common interest are converging. Hundreds of examples, large and small, demonstrate how social, ethical, and financial concerns are blending as we become more function-driven. In the past the interests of those at the bottom of the pyramid were in conflict with those at the top. Today, enlightened employers know that it is to their advantage to have the best educated and most satisfied workforce possible. These leaders understand that their futures rest on the shoulders of their employees.

This shift in thinking is taking place in every field. I recently worked with a major telemarketing firm that was seeking national legislation to regulate telemarketing and outlaw fraud and nuisance practices. In the past it would have been unheard of for an industry leader to support federal regulation. Such a company would have been more likely to exploit its position for all it was worth financially, regardless of the human costs. But because this company has taken a long-term view, it understands that abuses by telemarketers who promote late-night 900-numbers or use computers to call consumers at dinnertime are giving the industry a sleazy reputation. So in its own economic interest, as well as in the public interest, this telemarketing firm is doing what would have been unheard of in the past — it is seeking national legislation to ensure high standards in its own industry.

Some organizations that verbalize function-driven ethics for marketing or public relations purposes end up committed to their verbiage. So it was with one corporate client of mine. The company initially made certain environmental decisions because it feared lawsuits and negative publicity, but over time it became genuinely concerned about the pollution it was causing. Deciding to go beyond image, it searched for ways to become more efficient and environmentally friendly. Over the course of several years, the company changed its manufacturing process to reduce pollution, initiated research into safer products and processes, adopted several environmentally oriented nonprofit organizations, and dedicated a percentage of profits from certain product lines to environmental causes!

The transition to a new global ethic is also taking place in the public sector. It can be witnessed in government, the arts, education, and nonprofit organizations. Ronald J. Areglado, assistant executive director of programs for the National Association of Elementary School Principals, recently described to me an aspect of this new balanced focus on ethics as it is developing in education:

It's important to give students the option to challenge their values. People who learn to think and can examine the implications of their behavior will develop values that they can live with. It is not the responsibility of the school to impose a set of values, but it is the school's responsibility to provide a framework and context for students to examine ethical questions so that they become thoughtful, caring human beings.

Every subject — math, science, art, history — is filled with values questions. People become more empowered by being encouraged to be more thoughtful about ethics questions.

Some visionary organizations have modeled function-driven ethics for years. It used to be said that what was good for General Motors was good for the nation, but today, McDonald's employs more people in this country than does GM — and, although not perfect, demonstrates the emerging global ethic. When mobs burned South Central Los Angeles in April 1992, *Time* magazine reported:

...hundreds of businesses, many of them black owned, had been destroyed. Yet not a single McDonald's restaurant had been torched. Within hours after the curfew was lifted, all South Central's Golden Arches were back up and running, feeding fire fighters, police and National Guard troops as well as burned-out citizens. The St. Thomas Aquinas Elementary School, with 300 hungry students and no utilities, called for lunches and got them free — with delivery to boot.

McDonald's president and CEO Edward H. Rensi was not surprised. "Our businesses there are owned by African American entrepreneurs who hired African American managers who hired African American employees who served everybody in the community, whether they were Korean, African American, or Caucasian." This is not just luck or chance; it is the result of a long-standing McDonald's policy that its stores reflect the communities in which they operate. As a result, nearly 70 percent of McDonald's restaurant managers and 25 percent of its executives are minorities and women, and so are about half of its corporate department heads.

Rensi credits Ray Kroc, the energetic salesman who forged the chain back in the 1950s, for its enlightened social policies. Kroc insisted that owners and managers become involved in community affairs, saying, "If you are going to take money out of a community, give something back. It's only good business." Since 1979, McDonald's has held affirmative-action seminars for its executives and managers. Employees have created programs such as McJobs, which has trained and employed 7,000 mentally and physically impaired employees, and McPride, which keeps students in school and rewards them for academic achievement while they work. McMasters is a program to hire older people, who give the stores a family-like feeling and set an example of caring, courtesy, and responsibility for younger employees. McDonald's store owners also developed a program that established 153 Ronald McDonald Houses, where families of seriously ill children can stay while the children undergo extensive medical treatment.

Perhaps the greatest impact McDonald's has had on the values of modern America has been through its job-training system. Its 8,800 U.S. restaurants train American youth of every hue. "Sending a kid to the Army used to be the standard way to teach kids values, discipline, respect for authority, to be a member of a team, get to work on time, brush your teeth, comb your hair, clean your fingernails," says Rensi. "Now, somehow, McDonald's has become the new entry-level job-training institution in America. We find ourselves doing things in that role that we would never imagine we would do."

Interestingly, McDonald's is one of the leading exporters of these values and principles. It has 3,600 restaurants overseas, from Beijing to Barcelona, where I recently bought a McPollo Sandwich from a smiling attendant who exhibited the courtesy, cleanliness, and efficiency that McDonald's employees everywhere are taught. It is almost like a capitalist Peace Corps, reaching out to different lands and people and showing them what function-driven cooperation toward common goals can produce.

McDonald's, like other forward-thinking organizations, has recognized that good behavior is good business. As a result, it has eliminated styrofoam cartons made with CFCs, which destroy the ozone layer. Strategic environmental thinking is emerging as a way that companies like McDonald's can improve the quality of their products, keep prices down, and support environmental issues.

One of the most dramatic stories of a happy marriage between doing the right thing and doing things right, especially concerning the environment, belongs to Anita Roddick, founder of The Body Shop, which, according to *Business Week* magazine, promotes "causes along with cosmetics." The company's 620 stores communicate a concern for the environment and for social issues, offering recyclable bottles and such items as soap in the shape of endangered species. It donates a percentage of profits to environmental and human rights groups and insists its leaders be active in local issues.

More and more leaders like Roddick are speaking out about ethics and standing on their principles. Steven S. Reinemund is forthright about defining a corporate vision for ethics. He is not afraid, as business leaders of the last several decades have been, to define what he is looking for in employees in terms of ethics. He says, "For me, the most important quality is not the intelligence to analyze complex strategies, the charm or perseverance to sell, or the discipline to manage far-flung operating systems. Before anything else, I look for strength of character — integrity."

In the form-driven world of the past, corporations driven by the profit motive sometimes conducted their business in a less than ethical manner. They then tried to ease their consciences and improve their public images by giving money to worthy causes through their corporate foundations. Today such divisions seem artificial. In the highly competitive global marketplace, organizations must conduct business in more ethical, humane, and environmentally sensitive ways. Their philanthropic arms should not be used for damage control but as a way to expand companies' contributions to society.

An increasing number of corporations are discovering that good ethics make good business. For example, Bavarian Motor Works — BMW — responding to German environmental legislation, designed its Z-1 sports car for easy disassembly, so that when its driving life is over all of its parts can be reused or recycled. Its simplicity decreases assembly and repair time and causes less waste. Sharpe, a Biddeford, Maine, manufacturer of audio and video cassettes, simplified its production process, resulting in major reductions in energy consumption, packaging, and pollution and production of a cassette that is higher in quality and lower in cost than that of its competition. Baldrige Award-winners Xerox and AT&T both link environmentalism to their continuous improvement programs, seeing the two as inextricably linked. Arthur Soderberg, manager of quality for corporate environment and safety engineering at AT&T, concludes, "If you have defects in processes creating waste or worker hazards, why not use the same processes that you [use] to solve quality problems? After all, waste or worker safety hazards usually indicate a deficiency in employee training or equipment that also affects quality."

There are many more examples of how businesses are acting in the public interest for their own economic benefit. Toys-R-Us decided to stop selling realistic toy guns. More than 170 American corporations sold their holdings in South Africa as a result of apartheid. Many cosmetic and pharmaceutical firms have halted animal testing. All of these moves are astute responses to consumer pressure; they are also good marketing strategies, because many people will buy a product, and even pay a bit more, if they believe they are supporting a group that shares their global ethic.

As private individuals, public figures, or organizational leaders, we can prepare for the 21st century by laying a solid ethical foundation. Each one of us must strive to be ethically consistent in all areas of our lives, whether we are acting in the personal, professional, or civic realm. Without a strong global ethic, all other efforts, no matter how skillful and informed, are bound to fail.

CHAPTER FIFTEEN

Exercising Empowerment

The truly great leaders of the past all had a keen sense of efficacy. They believed they could make a difference and inspired others to believe that they mattered. Whether these great leaders promoted form-driven structures, like John D. Rockefeller and General George Patton, or challenged the inequities of the form-driven structure, like Mohandas Gandhi and Martin Luther King, Jr., they believed they could make a difference — and they inspired others to take action.

Empowerment is often thought of as something leaders do to others, as in, "Let's empower our volunteers...." Ultimately, empowerment can only come from within individuals and groups. But it can be encouraged by wise leaders who create and support an environment in which others can grow.

We have entered a period in which many people all over the world are craving opportunities to be more involved in decisions that affect them. Effective leaders today recognize this need and provide mechanisms for their constituents to participate actively in the formation and attainment of common goals. This is in sharp contrast to the last few decades, when an alarming number of Americans disengaged from civic and social action.

On a questionnaire I have given to thousands of senior executives in the federal government, one item asks respondents to indicate whether they think the following statement is possible, probable, or preferable: "By the year 2000 federal workers will be encouraged to be risk-takers, innovative, and creative." An overwhelming percentage of every group — at least 90 percent — respond that they think these qualities are desirable in the federal workplace. Yet the same percentage report that they do not think that it is probable that these qualities will be encouraged. And more than 90 percent say they believe that such a scenario is *not even possible!*

One has to wonder about a system where a resounding majority of top executives report that they think a behavior is detrimental and would like to see it changed but believe it never will be changed. Do these employees see themselves as passive and powerless, accepting norms promulgated by a large, insensitive, organization? Or do they claim that they want organizational behavior to change but not really mean it? After all, many people find it more comfortable to complain about not being allowed to be creative and innovative than to change their behavior.

As the 1990s unfold, more and more people are coming to understand the fast pace of change in the world and, rather than holding back in fear or self-interest, are demanding a more active role in helping their institutions define and achieve goals. They are recognizing that their interests are not separate from everyone else's but are intricately interconnected. They understand and want to counteract the negative impact that hollow empowerment efforts of the past may have created.

Many of us have experienced the frustration and sense of betrayal that come with accepting an invitation to participate in decisions, only to discover that our views are not really wanted or respected. Real empowerment comes only in an environment of mutual trust. People must value each other's contributions to pursuing common goals. Such efforts take commitment, time, and resources — three things usually in short supply but nonetheless required if organizations are to gear up for the 21st century. And many leaders are beginning to make the commitment, contribute the time, and provide the resources. A growing number of organizations are fostering a sense of efficacy and participation among their employees.

Leaders in every industry are making a genuine effort to empower their people. Jan Carlzon, president of Scandinavian Airlines, has been known for more than a decade for his commitment to employee empowerment. He likes to tell the story of a business traveler who left his ticket in his hotel room but was able to board his plane because the ticket agent had the authority to solve the problem on the spot. Carlzon encourages other leaders to understand the importance of recognizing their employees as decision makers who need the freedom to solve problems for customers. He stresses, "An individual without information cannot take responsibility; an individual who is given information cannot help but take responsibility."

William McCarten, president of Host International Travel Plazas by Marriott, agrees with Carlzon. As he told me:

> A few people sitting in the executive offices cannot really drive success. What we have to do is find better ways of motivating our organization.
>
> Change is inevitable, leading to a highly charged, uncertain atmosphere in our industry. We must move away from autocratic management and become more innovative. We've got to improve customer satisfaction. I know of no better way to do that than through our associates and employees out there in the field. They have contact with our customers every day. We've got to communicate our strategies to them clearly so that they can participate in strengthening our organization. The secret is to be sure that we have people who feel they can take risks and have a valuable role in the success of this business.

McCarten tries to put this philosophy into practice through activities and programs designed to improve communication and employee involvement in decisions that affect them.

When the National Education Association (NEA) formed the National Center for Innovation, its senior director, Gary Watts, decided to practice what the center preached. One of his first tasks was to focus on empowering staff members, most of whom had worked their entire careers in form-driven institutions. According to Watts, they had to change their mindset about everything.

Starting with something as seemingly inconsequential as staff meetings, employees had to learn completely new roles. They took turns facilitating, keeping time, and serving as "worriers," guiding projects along to completion. Tasks were not assigned by job titles but by interest, need, and skill. Explains Watts, "Managers do regular work here. They are part of the work team and can be junior members of a team. Their rank is irrelevant."

In addition to finding they needed lengthier staff meetings, the employees also found they needed fast, effective ways to communicate regarding the work of the center. For example, a brief stand-up staff meeting is now convened once a week for the purpose of "touching base" with colleagues — to get updates on individuals' activities and on the status of various projects. These meetings have promoted a more congenial climate.

Another idea that the center's teams implemented was *credentialing.* When they were charged by the NEA to increase the center's credibility outside the NEA community, all center staff members selected substantive areas in which they wanted to become recognized experts. With the help of colleagues, they constructed plans to develop that expertise. Today, center employees are frequently called on by leading organizations to address topics they specialize in, a testimony to the success of their ongoing credentialing efforts. Watts adds, "Our credentialing process has added an element of personal growth as well as organizational advantage. Our staff is proud of the advances it has made in the many innovative issue areas it has tackled."

Without mentors to nurture and encourage them, most people must discover their own unique contribution to society. Consider the case of Alfred Nobel, creator of the Nobel Prize for Peace. For most of his life, Nobel was not considered by contemporaries to be a noble man. A manufacturer of dynamite, he was reported to be a cruel employer and a ruthless man. Michael Evlanoff and Marjorie Fluor, in their book *Alfred Nobel: The Loneliest Millionaire,* reported how Nobel's life was turned upside down one day as he read the obituary of his brother Ludwig:

When Ludwig died and Alfred read the obituary, written by a French journalist, he received a psychic wound so deep, so mortal, that he could never recover from it. The journalist had mistaken the death of Ludwig for that of Alfred and had reviewed Alfred's life, proclaiming him "the merchant of death."

This label shocked and saddened Alfred. He wondered whether in truth he deserved any other recognition. Had he done anything for suffering humanity, except to bequeath it these weapons of destruction?

As a result of the self-examination that followed, Alfred Nobel changed his life so dramatically that when he did die, his obituary described him as a humanitarian, a leader, and a visionary. Establishing the Nobel Prize for Peace is one of the many steps he took to redirect his life and his resources.

Like Alfred Nobel, we all need to ask ourselves what legacy we are leaving behind. Harry Emerson Fosdick, a well-known religious leader of the 1940s and 1950s, posed a timely and timeless question when he asked, "Am I more a part of the problem or a part of the solution?" If we do not believe we can make a difference, we will never try; if we never try, we will never succeed. If we believe that we cannot change the way things are, our perception becomes reality: we will never emerge from the cocoon of self-imposed powerlessness.

As we enter the 21st century, organizations will be able to accomplish less and less without the genuine involvement of all stakeholders. Leaders will be needed at the community, organizational, national, and international levels who not only

Never doubt that a small group of thoughtful, committed citizens can change the world; indeed, it's the only thing that ever has.
MARGARET MEAD

There is no history, only biography.
RALPH WALDO EMERSON

believe they can make a difference, but can also encourage others to actively pursue their visions.

We need to create environments where people feel empowered. We must offer to a wider range of participants the opportunity to share leadership and improve decision making. And we need to help young people learn that their voices matter.

CHAPTER SIXTEEN

Being Propelled by Purpose

When I was a very young girl, a friend of the family had a nervous breakdown. I clearly remember my fright and confusion after we visited her in the hospital one Sunday afternoon. In the car on the way home, I asked my father what caused nervous breakdowns and whether anyone could get them. He replied that people who had nervous breakdowns had lost two important things in their lives: belief in something larger than themselves and a sense of humor. He assured me that if I kept those two things, I would not suffer a breakdown as our family friend had. All these years later, I still remember his formula and wonder how many individuals and organizations might have prevented breakdowns if they had held onto those two simple ingredients.

No single factor distinguishes successful individuals and organizations from unsuccessful ones as much as a sense of purpose. If you think of any of the people or organizations you greatly admire, you will find that they all have one thing in common — a purpose that involves serving others. They believe that their lives or their company's goals are first about giving and then about getting.

Because great people and organizations believe they have a purpose larger than their own needs, they do not place themselves at the center of their universe. They serve other people and "ideas whose time has come," valuing something more encompassing than their own desires and whims. With this broader perspective, they are able to take themselves and their day-to-day trials and tribulations less seriously. They can laugh more easily at themselves and their predicaments than those who place themselves at the epicenter of importance. Like a boat with a deep keel, they can stay on course in rough, stormy waters more easily than those whose ballast is all at surface level.

People and organizations that are guided by their sense of purpose are very effective in a rapidly changing world. Because they define their existence in terms of a vision and their role in making that vision a reality, they are not easily thrown by the ups and downs of day-to-day life. Their goal may be something as prosaic as "providing the most reliable housecleaning service in the city," but when it is felt with conviction and commitment, it guides their daily behavior. People and organizations that have clarity about their purpose are less likely than others to get sidetracked by low-priority demands on their time. And they are more likely to find inner and external resources to achieve their goals.

Many function-driven individuals and organizations like to develop a vision statement. Vision statements are compelling descriptions of what we want the future to be like. They can be from a personal, family, organizational, community, national, or global perspective. They come from the heart as well as the head and describe what we want the future to look, sound, and feel like. They often include a time frame in which the vision will be realized.

Vision statements are supported by goals. Goals describe the major components of the vision so that when the goals are accomplished, the vision has been attained. The number of goals needed to realize a vision varies, but the general rule is that the fewer goals there are, the more likely they are to be achieved. Even multinational corporations restrict the number of major goals they set to no more than seven. They find that if they set too many major goals, they are less likely to achieve any of them, having diluted their energy by directing it in too many directions. Like visions, goals should address *what* we would like to see happen, not *how* we intend to achieve them. In other words, both visions and goals describe the destination, not the journey.

Articulating visions and goals is important for both groups and individuals. Organizations of all kinds are engaging in strategic planning, Total Quality Management, and other endeavors that depend on visualization and goal-setting. These efforts are most productive when leaders are open to building consensus around a shared vision, when participants are willing to take the time such a process requires, when expected outcomes are clear, and when effective facilitation is provided.

The way a vision or goal is developed or articulated can clearly inhibit or facilitate its attainment. Over the years, people have studied effective visualization and goal-setting techniques to determine what makes some more successful than others. The following set of guidelines, which apply equally well to organizations and individuals, summarize the characteristics of effective visions and goals.

1. Choose worthy visions and goals.

Our visions and goals should challenge us to perform at peak levels. Worthy visions and goals require us to act consistently with our highest beliefs and values.

Whenever we fail to select visions and goals that merit our attention, we are bound to lose. During a workshop on career goal-setting, one participant set a goal to have her manager's superiors recognize his incompetence. In spite of warnings that negative goals are invariably counterproductive, she proceeded to develop an intricate plan for trapping, embarrassing, and humiliating her managerial adversary. About a year later, I heard that she had indeed succeeded in her goal: her boss had taken early retirement. But attaining that goal had extracted a far greater toll on her than on him. He had been able to retire at a young age with a good compensation package and had become a well-paid consultant. She, however, had become consumed by her obsession to "get him" and had dropped out of graduate school, lost many friends at work, and become bitter and frustrated. The greatest irony was that she had lost any chance for advancement in her organization by the time she accomplished her negative goal.

Most people can distinguish visions and goals that are consistent with their highest values from those that are not. Adhering to the highest visions and goals, even when reality strains against them, promotes greatness. The core of Winston Churchill's genius was his steadfast ability to retain clear and lofty visions and goals even in the face of grim reality. In 1940, Churchill shared his vision with his country:

What General Weygand called the Battle of France is over. I expect that the Battle of Britain is about to begin. Upon this battle depends the survival of Christian civilization. Upon it depends our own British life and the long continuity of our institutions and our Empire. The whole fury and might of the enemy must very soon be turned on us. Hitler knows that he will have to break us in this island or lose the war. If we can stand up to him all Europe may be free and the life of the world may move forward into broad, sunlit uplands; but if we fail then the whole world, including the United States, and all that we have known and cared for, will sink into the abyss of a new dark age made more sinister, and perhaps more prolonged, by the lights of a perverted science. Let us therefore brace ourselves to our duty, and so bear ourselves that, if the British Commonwealth and its Empire lasts for a thousand years, men will say, "This was their finest hour."

Churchill not only held to his highest convictions, he communicated his vision in such a compelling manner that he inspired others to believe it could be realized. Visions and goals that challenge us have a power unmatched by those that address lesser accomplishments.

2. Consider the fullest range of possibilities imaginable.

As we become more knowledgeable about a discipline or more settled in an organization, we learn to adopt its belief system. Within its environment, certain things are believed to be possible; others are not. Often, the range of options considered possible is much narrower than it needs to be. If people think something is impossible, they will not try to do it, and, of course, it therefore remains undone. From their point of view, it is indeed impossible.

In establishing visions and goals, it is essential to remove all barriers to what we or others think might be possible — to be able to "dream the impossible dream." When Orville and Wilbur Wright were building their first airplane in 1903, the best scientific and technical minds in the world insisted that a heavier-than-air machine could not sustain itself in flight. Undaunted by ridicule, the Wright brothers clung to their impossible vision — with well-known results.

Today, scores of people are accomplishing things that their doctors, parents, teachers, or others told them were impossible. Rick Allen, a drummer with the rock band Def Leppard, lost one arm and severely injured the other in an auto accident. But he returned to his group and has the distinction of becoming the industry's only one-armed professional drummer.

Baseball player Jim Abbott, who is missing a hand, was the winning pitcher in the United States' championship 1988 Olympic baseball game against Japan. He says about his remarkable talent, "I just learned to play with one hand." In 1993, he even pitched a no-hitter for the New York Yankees!

For generations of runners, a four-minute mile was impossible. Then, in 1954, Roger Bannister ran a mile in under four minutes, shattering a long-held belief that had been elevated to an absolute "truth." Once that barrier was broken, running a mile in less than four minutes became routine. Today it is not even noteworthy.

If visions and goals are required to be "possible" — meaning *practical* or *realistic* — they will never possess the creative energy to motivate action. Mediocrity is not inspiring. In creating visions and goals, it is vital to consider the full range of possibilities.

Sometimes we restrict our range of options by artificially creating two extreme choices that appear to be mutually exclusive. We believe that, in order to get one choice, the other must be sacrificed. These are the only options we will consider.

For example, one of my neighbors was unhappy in his marriage, so he established the goal of living alone. He had come to equate unhappiness with living with another person. He therefore perceived only two opposing alternatives: being unhappily married or happily living alone. He did not consider the possibility that one could be happy living with another person or unhappy living alone.

Similarly, the CEO of a large organization told his marketing staff that if sales continued to decline in the next quarter, he would be compelled to close down the department. He set up an artificial either/or situation and failed to consider a wider range of options. Because the lead time on the work this department had undertaken was far longer than three months, its ambitious projects had not yielded results by his deadline. The CEO said he regretted having to fire his marketing director and reassign the staff but was forced to do so by their inability to meet his terms. Unfortunately, his organization's financial health suffered as a result of his self-imposed forced choice.

3. State visions and goals in positive terms.

Vision and goal statements should address the positive things we want. They are doomed when they are formulated in terms of what we do not want. When we focus on NOT smoking, NOT being late, or NOT being in debt, we are actually drawing our attention to the very thing we say we do not want. Every parent knows that as soon as children are told, "Don't spill the milk," they do. That's because their brains record this command as, "Spill the milk — don't." By the time the "don't" is recorded, it's too late; they have already done it.

Adult minds work the same way. Focusing on what we do not want just draws attention and energy toward the negative. Goals should always be stated in the affirmative. They are far more potent when they engender positive images of what we DO want for ourselves. For example, setting a goal to become the best in our field or to surpass our past performance will always yield better results than setting a goal to beat a certain competitor or *not* lose market share.

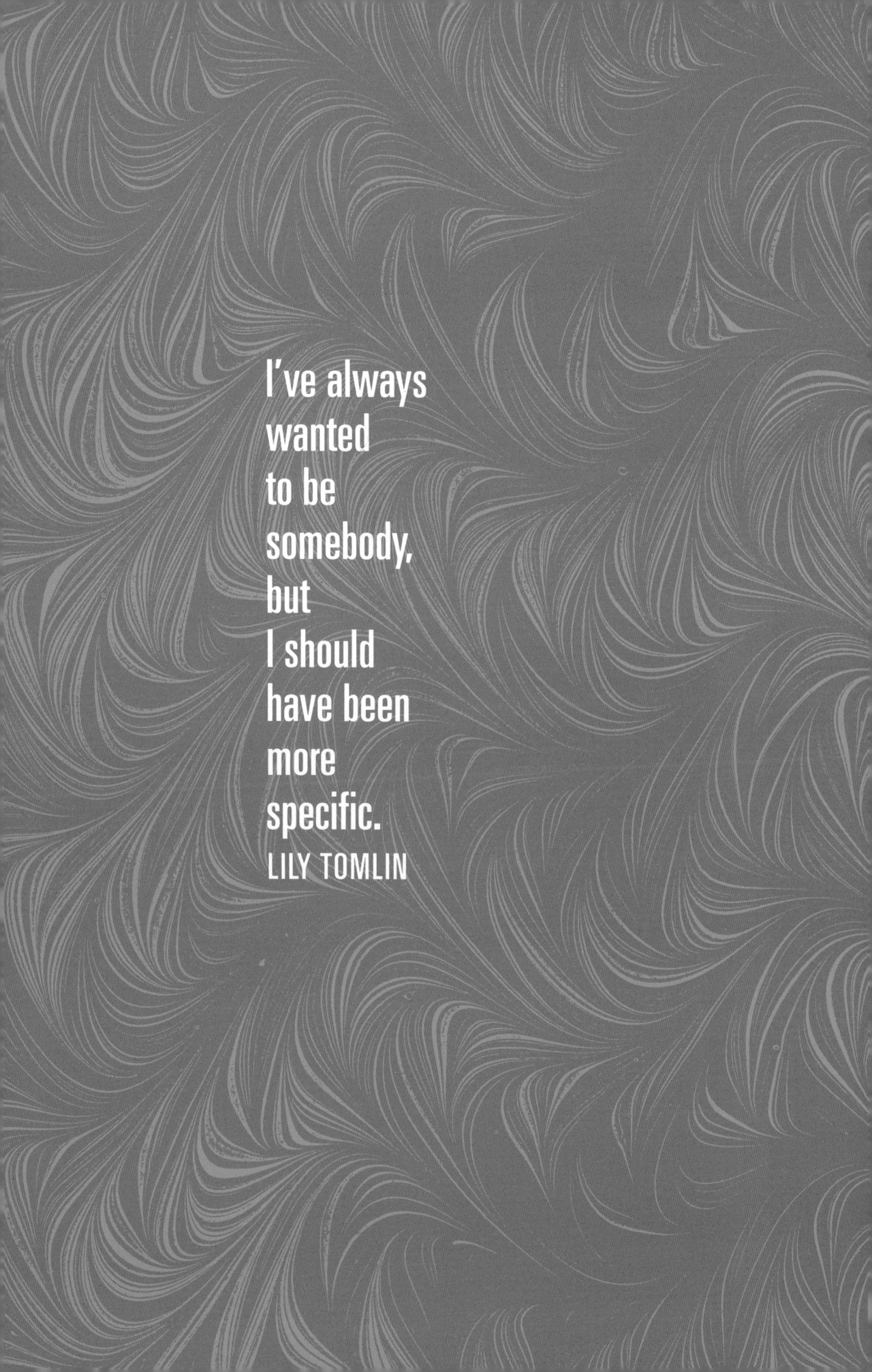

I've always
wanted
to be
somebody,
but
I should
have been
more
specific.
LILY TOMLIN

4. Distinguish genuine goals from what society, family, the media, advertising, and others say we should want.

A group of managers at a goal-setting retreat built a collage of what they wanted for the future, cutting out and assembling pictures and words from magazines as a visual representation of their corporate vision. Predominant among the images were dollar bills, scantily clad women, snowmobiles, and alcoholic beverages. As they reflected on those icons during the subsequent discussion, these managers admitted that as "red-blooded males," they felt compelled to include such items, but were not committed to them as goals. They concluded that "society," via advertising and the media, encouraged them to think that this was what they were supposed to want.

Advertising has so influenced contemporary thinking that we often do not realize the extent to which subliminal suggestions shape our visions. Because the products and lifestyle choices incessantly pitched by merchandisers unconsciously influence our desires, we must be clear about what we really want — define our *real* goals. Such clarity forces us to root out superficial, idle fantasies and redirects our attention to goals that are aimed at meaningful growth and achievement. We are able to separate our real visions from societal and commercial fixations.

These external standards are so pervasive and come from so many directions that it is hard to know which standards are our own. The pressures to conform are tremendous. Many women still feel incomplete if they are not married. Young girls become anorexic or bulimic because they are certain that people will like them only if they are thin. Some companies become convinced that what they need in order to pull out of their economic slump is a more impressive headquarters building. Many city councils, responding to political stimuli, continue to focus on peripheral, cosmetic issues to avoid addressing difficult, core problems.

Without the maturity and broader perspective to distinguish between what we want for ourselves and what others think we should want, we will have limited success in establishing meaningful visions and goals.

5. Distinguish between means and ends.

A common error in defining visions and goals is to confuse means with ends. It is important to ask, "Are these our ultimate goals? Or are they merely a means toward achieving our ultimate goals?" If the answer is the latter, then the focus must be on the final thing we want, not the intermediate step. The likelihood of reaching our final goals is restricted considerably if we focus our attention on the means of achieving them rather than on what they are.

A participant in a seminar on personal goal-setting asserted that her goal was to acquire lots of money. After further questioning, she revealed that she was not so much interested in the money for its own sake; she wanted money so she could be free to travel. Once she focused her attention on her ultimate goal of travel, opportunities to do so, many of which required little or no money, appeared everywhere. She represented a community organization at a national conference in San Francisco, an opportunity she would have missed had her attention still been on money. Once there, she joined the group's international task force that would be meeting in Helsinki the following year. When her church choir discussed its annual summer tour of other churches in the state, she suggested they research touring Europe, a trip they made just six months later with her as their leader. All of this happened only after she shifted her attention from the means to the end she really wanted.

6. Describe the complete results desired.

Too often we fall short of describing the full results we want. This happens either because we are afraid we might not achieve them or because we are thinking too small.

A colleague was telling me that what she really wanted was to get her new book published. When pressed about whether that was all she wanted, she stopped, thought for a moment, and then replied, "No. Not only do I want it published, I want it to be financially successful — and I want the critics to love it." She looked up and grinned; it was the first time she had articulated her complete vision for the book, even to herself.

A young couple looking for a new house made a list of all the characteristics of their ideal home. They found a place that had every single item on their list and quickly made an offer on it. Only after they moved in did they realize that they had overlooked some very important qualities. For example, "quiet" had not been on their list, because they had never before lived around the corner from a fire station, bars, and nightclubs. They are now dealing with the noisy consequences of having pursued and achieved an incomplete vision.

An organization may set a goal to develop a strategic plan but may fail to specify that it should be created through collaboration. Or it may not link the results of the strategic plan to improving the quality or volume of its business. By focusing on only part of a complete vision, organizations and individuals often omit other results that are equally important.

7. Intentionally choose a future direction rather than allow yourself to drift into it.

Intellectually, we know that *not* choosing a course of action is, in itself, a choice. Yet too often we continue to abdicate responsibility for our personal, professional, and civic lives by choosing to maintain the status quo. To continue to smoke or gain weight is as much a choice as selecting the healthier alternative; it is just a passive decision. To continue to have poor communication with family members or colleagues at work is to select that pattern, if only unconsciously. To refrain from voting, for whatever reason, is to participate in the selection of those who govern. In establishing visions and goals, it is important to recognize that to abstain from making intentional choices is to choose by default.

Taking deliberate action can be much more difficult than maintaining the status quo. But even maintaining the status quo is still *doing something*. Not setting goals and visions does not mean we are not acting. It simply means that our actions are unintentional and focused on the past rather than intentional and focused on the future.

We have countless excuses for not making proactive choices, among them uncertainty about which choice to make, insecurity about what lies ahead, and unwillingness to accept personal responsibility for our own decisions. For many, there can be psychological comfort in feeling like a victim or rationalizing that "the future is out of my hands." This comfort comes at too high a cost and reduces our effectiveness on both personal and organizational levels. Even genuine victims, long-term prisoners of war, report that one of the keys to survival is making a strong mental commitment to visions and holding on passionately to the belief that, even if we are not in control of all the conditions of our lives, we are responsible for how we perceive those conditions and what we do with them.

8. Make visions and goals free from unnecessary restrictions or conditions.

While visions and goals need to be complete, they should not include extraneous conditions. For example, a man enthusiastically reported to a confidant his "vision" for a life-long partner. "I want to find a woman who is petite, athletic, has nice nails and hair, went to a private school, is from the Midwest, likes classic cars, has traveled widely, is a great cook, has a nice singing voice and a great sense of humor, likes science fiction, and is wealthy." This may seem like a well-constructed vision in that it is clear, specific, and, if not complete, certainly comprehensive. The problem is that, unless all of those characteristics are really of equal and ultimate importance, this man is limiting the likelihood of finding a mate by placing unnecessary conditions on his vision. He may reject someone who meets most of his criteria but is missing a few visible but less critical ones. Or he may be so busy checking his list that he fails to notice other things that he has not listed (Is she intelligent? Is she sane? Is she heterosexual?).

  Like individuals, organizations sometimes need to be reminded that they should include only those conditions and characteristics that are absolutely necessary to define their goal. Sometimes we can visualize only one path to a goal. We should not impose that path on the goal itself, thus preventing its achievement in other ways. A pharmaceutical company, for example, might decide that it wants to be the leading provider of dental hygiene products. But if it specifies, without research, which one of its 14 products will make the company first in the dental hygiene market, it will surely miss opportunities its other products (or other potential products) might offer. It needlessly limits its vision by placing unnecessary conditions on it.

  The more conditions we place on visions, the less likely we are to attain them. Clearly defining which characteristics actually constitute the vision and which are tangential is critical to success.

9. Seeking goals sometimes requires living with discomfort.

Sometimes pursuing visions and goals requires a willingness to live with discomfort, at least for a little while. Too often, in order to fill a void, appear decisive, or reduce discomfort, we choose something less than what we really want.

  An acquaintance had long been talking about how unhappy she was with her position in a large international organization. For years she spoke wistfully about launching her own firm or linking up with a few other trainers in a collaborative venture. Due to unexpected budget cutbacks, she suddenly found herself unemployed but with a handsome severance agreement. Within the week, she received an offer from another large firm, a competitor of her previous employer, for essentially the same position she had just left. To reduce her feelings of anxiety, discomfort, and embarrassment caused by being unemployed, she accepted the offer without giving herself time to consider her true goals. Within a few months, she had the same complaints about her new employer as she had about the previous one.

  Establishing visions and goals requires having the courage to take whatever time is necessary to move through uncomfortable stages. I have seen new leaders enter organizations and immediately change things around, convinced that if they did not make changes early, they would lose the opportunity. Activity purely for its own sake is never productive. It is a sign that people are quickly trying to fill a perceived void rather than trusting themselves, their colleagues, and the process.

10. We must accept ultimate responsibility for the selection of our own goals.

There is nothing wrong with discussing our goals with others or seeking help in clarifying them. But we severely impair our ability to achieve our goals when we abdicate responsibility for setting them. Whenever we allow others to set goals on our behalf, we sacrifice personal power.

For example, someone I know was considering a divorce. For months, he kept asking his therapist and friends if he should leave his wife. He kept a running tally of how many said he should stay and how many said he should leave, as if somehow others should make the decision for him. When I ran into him years later, he reported that, so far, 145 people thought he should divorce his wife and 73 thought he should stay married!

Organizations, too, abdicate responsibility. In an effort to avoid taking risks or responsibility, some executives hire consultants to make their tough organizational decisions for them. They believe that they can hide behind the argument that, "The government/accountants/board/consultants made us do that." Some government agencies, for example, have come under attack in recent years for allowing contractors and other, more partisan branches of government to alter their goals and agendas.

11. Recognize that some things will happen to us that we did not choose.

It is important to realize that things can happen that were not sought. In Chapter 1, I emphasized that human choice is only one of the factors that shape the future. Chance also plays a role in determining what happens to us. Sometimes, in spite of our best efforts, we have bad luck.

Some self-actualization groups believe that whatever happens to us is self-induced. Although relatively harmless when things are going well, when we run into trouble, this mind-over-matter philosophy, which contends that on some level we have wished for negative things, is harmful. We need to recognize that we can take personal responsibility for our lives, but other factors also come into play.

This line of reasoning is used by people who believe that the poor want to be poor, the jobless do not want to work, the homeless like living on the street, and high school dropouts just do not care about getting ahead. When groups of disadvantaged people are scooped together into categories such as "the permanent underclass," they are conveniently depersonalized, creating an excuse for inattentiveness and inaction. Not too many years ago, a U.S. undersecretary of education believed that resources should not go to educating disabled children because, he asserted, they were God's special children, and *meant* to be that way!

12. Make sure that collective visions and goals are shared by all parties who have a stake in them.

All those who are included in or affected by a vision or goal need to participate in its development — or at least have an opportunity to say if they share it. Too often, mates, parents, employers, and elected officials set goals for others who are not represented in the goal-setting process. One organization recently got into trouble for just this reason. Its chairman and president, wanting to be as efficient as possible, wrote a vision statement for the organization and then distributed it to staff members. Although the staff members may have developed an identical statement had they wrestled with the task themselves, they were so annoyed at being excluded from the process that they revolted and refused to rubber stamp someone else's vision.

Compare that experience with a school district I guided through the strategic planning process. Its superintendent was determined to include all stakeholders in the community in establishing its vision and goals. So many community leaders responded positively to his invitation that the group grew to 300, meeting over the course of several months. With a focused, open agenda, the process resulted in powerful vision and goal statements that all 300 participants proudly "owned."

13. Keep visions and goals current, revisiting them frequently and revising them when necessary.

In a rapidly changing world, it is essential to make sure that our visions and goals are current. Because so many factors can cause instant and dramatic changes in our situations, we need to be constantly reevaluating what we want. It is far better to revise or even reject outdated goals than to continue to pursue them.

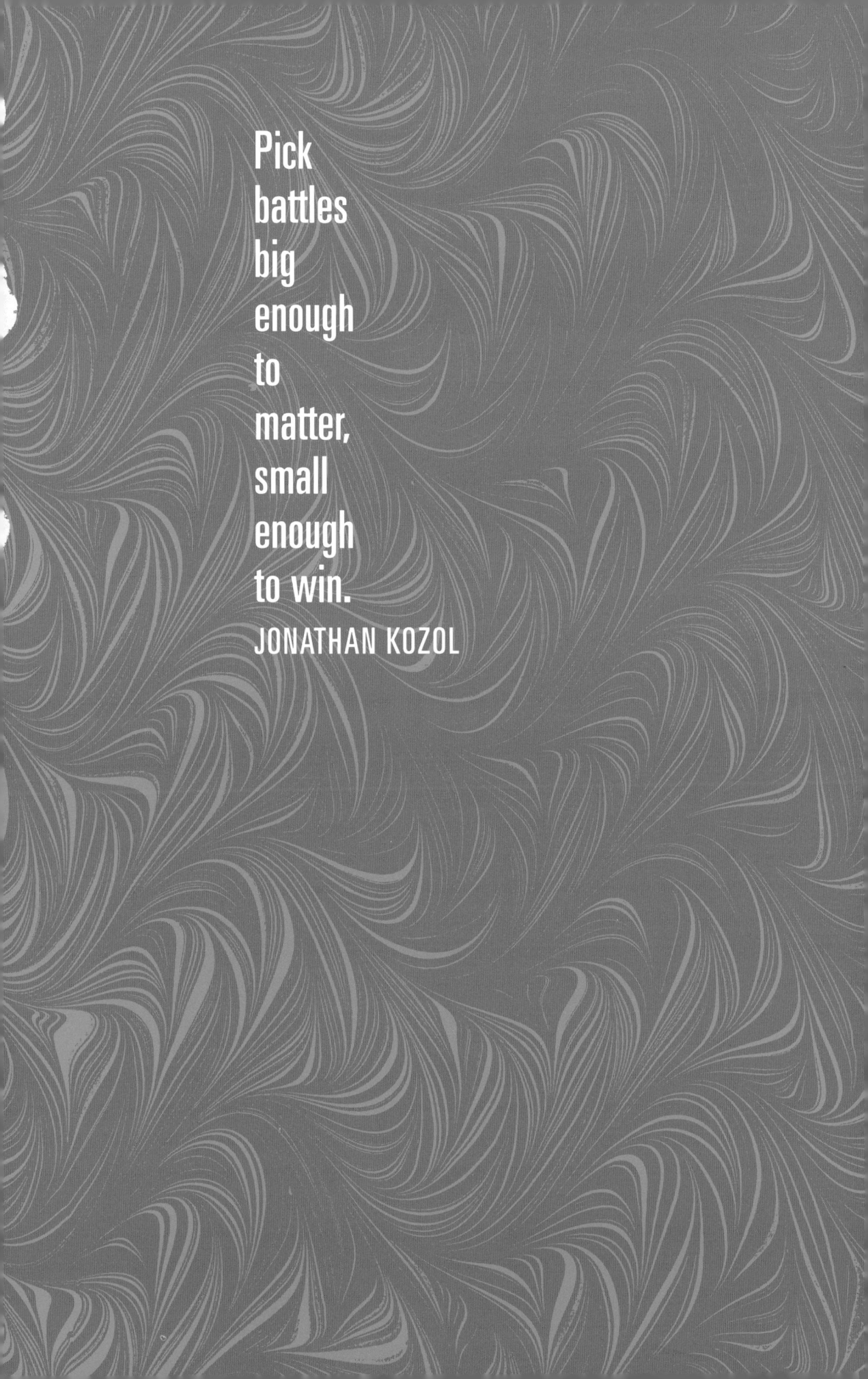

Pick battles big enough to matter, small enough to win.
JONATHAN KOZOL

The pursuit of visions and goals provides new information and insights that should be used to refine our ideas about what we want for the future. For example, a large nonprofit organization that kept checking its "current reality" noticed that the market for its services was changing. It rapidly developed new services to meet the needs of its emerging clientele. This ability to adjust goals to changing environments allowed the organization to succeed when others failed.

Focusing on mission and goals is vital for leaders who want to successfully lead into the 21st century. It energizes and unites people. It clarifies the *what, why,* and *how* questions that dominate contemporary life. It allows us to maintain a creative tension between where we want to go and where we are and prevents us from getting sidetracked. And, most important, it helps us align our priorities and find the strength to fight for the ideas we most believe in.

Dispelling the megatrends myths requires the courage to develop and practice the function-driven leadership behaviors presented in this section. Each behavior fits with and supports the others so that leaders can help themselves and their organizations move successfully into the 21st century.

How Prepared Are You and Your Organization for the 21st Century?

PERSONAL/ORGANIZATIONAL INVENTORY

First rate YOURSELF. For each item, place an X on the top line of the scale above the number that reflects how you stand with regard to the statements on both sides of the scale. Then do the same for your ORGANIZATION. This time place an X beneath the bottom line of the scale for each item.

Note: By having different stakeholders complete the inventory, you can form a more complete portrait of your organization and yourself. You can also use the inventory to initiate discussions about what changes are needed in your organization.

I. Building a Long-Term, Global Perspective

A. The orientation is
   exclusively short term.　　-3 -2 -1 0 +1 +2 +3　　both short and long term.

B. The focus is mostly on
   immediate results that can be seen and easily measured.　　-3 -2 -1 0 +1 +2 +3　　short- and long-term results that may be invisible or difficult to measure.

C. There is a belief
   only in simple linear, cause-and-effect relationships.　　-3 -2 -1 0 +1 +2 +3　　in multiple, often complex and non-linear relationships.

D. Value is placed
   only on easily quantifiable factors.　　-3 -2 -1 0 +1 +2 +3　　on important factors whether or not they are easily quantifiable.

E. There is encouragement to
   remain separate, competitive, and suspicious.　　-3 -2 -1 0 +1 +2 +3　　cooperate and collaborate whenever possible.

F. The focus is on
   looking for the quick fix or easy payoff.　　-3 -2 -1 0 +1 +2 +3　　long-term investments, even if they are hard to measure in the short term.

G. Decisions are based on
   how they will affect only the decision makers.　　-3 -2 -1 0 +1 +2 +3　　how they will affect everyone involved.

H. Major decisions are based on
   isolated, incomplete data.　　-3 -2 -1 0 +1 +2 +3　　the context and patterns of information.

II. Concentrating on Quality

A. Suggestions for improvement are
    ignored or discouraged.   -3 -2 -1 0 +1 +2 +3   rewarded and encouraged.

B. Standards are set that
    accept mediocrity.   -3 -2 -1 0 +1 +2 +3   reward excellence.

C. Decision making is
    centralized.   -3 -2 -1 0 +1 +2 +3   decentralized.

D. The emphasis is on
    rules and structure.   -3 -2 -1 0 +1 +2 +3   process and results.

E. Standards are
    unclear and not valued.   -3 -2 -1 0 +1 +2 +3   clear and valued.

F. The opportunities for skill development and professional growth are
    few or none.   -3 -2 -1 0 +1 +2 +3   plentiful.

G Feedback is sought
    only from those who reinforce current practices.   -3 -2 -1 0 +1 +2 +3   from different groups, including those who may disagree with or question current practices.

III. Encouraging Innovation

A. Important decisions are based on
    what did/did not work in the past.   -3 -2 -1 0 +1 +2 +3   what might work in the future.

B. Decisions are made to
    avoid or discourage risk-taking.   -3 -2 -1 0 +1 +2 +3   encourage and reward appropriate risk-taking.

C. The primary value is on
uniformity.   -3 -2 -1 0 +1 +2 +3   creativity.

D. Management style can most accurately
be described as bureaucratic, rigid, and rule-oriented.   -3 -2 -1 0 +1 +2 +3   entrepreneurial, flexible, and customer-oriented.

E. Failure is
buried, ignored, or punished.   -3 -2 -1 0 +1 +2 +3   learned from and built on.

F. Problems are
accepted as previously defined or as defined by others.   -3 -2 -1 0 +1 +2 +3   redefined and viewed in light of new conditions.

G. Solutions to major problems usually
miss the core issue or address only symptoms.   -3 -2 -1 0 +1 +2 +3   address core issues and potential causes.

IV. Improving Cooperation and Communication

A. There is a tendency to
hoard information.   -3 -2 -1 0 +1 +2 +3   share information.

B. Customers, clients, and nonmanagement employees are
prevented from having the same information as decision makers.   -3 -2 -1 0 +1 +2 +3   provided all available information.

C. Staff are
discouraged from working with other units or other organizations.   -3 -2 -1 0 +1 +2 +3   encouraged to work with other units or other organizations.

D. The views of nonmanagement employees, customers, and other interested parties is
never valued.   -3 -2 -1 0 +1 +2 +3   always valued.

E. Decisions are made
on a reactive basis without input from a variety of sources.   -3 -2 -1 0 +1 +2 +3   proactively, with input from a variety of sources.

V. Committing to Ethical Practices

A. The interests of all affected parties are
    ignored or minimized. -3 -2 -1 0 +1 +2 +3 valued and respected.

B. Environmental consequences of decisions are
    ignored or minimized. -3 -2 -1 0 +1 +2 +3 taken into account.

C. Racial, ethnic, gender, and lifestyle differences are
    a basis for discrimination. -3 -2 -1 0 +1 +2 +3 respected and valued.

D. Employees are
    expected to increase their efforts without commensurate rewards. -3 -2 -1 0 +1 +2 +3 valued and compensated fairly for their contributions.

E. Public communications, sales claims, and financial reporting are
    deceptive. -3 -2 -1 0 +1 +2 +3 honest.

VI. Exercising Empowerment

A. Employees believe they are
    unappreciated and underutilized. -3 -2 -1 0 +1 +2 +3 appreciated and wisely utilized.

B. Employees feel they have
    little freedom in making day-to-day decisions about their jobs. -3 -2 -1 0 +1 +2 +3 freedom in making day-to-day decisions about their jobs.

C. Employees, customers, and other relevant individuals feel
    personally removed from the organization's future. -3 -2 -1 0 +1 +2 +3 personally invested in the future of the organization.

D. Decisions are made
    by the person with the most authority. -3 -2 -1 0 +1 +2 +3 by the person with the most information.

E. Public communications, sales claims, and financial reporting are
    deceptive. -3 -2 -1 0 +1 +2 +3 honest.

VII. Being Propelled by Purpose

A. **In pursuing goals, externally imposed conditions and restrictions are**

accepted or used as an excuse for inactivity.   -3 -2 -1 0 +1 +2 +3   challenged and redefined.

B. **Decisions are**

reactive.   -3 -2 -1 0 +1 +2 +3   proactive.

C. **The mission and goals are**

unclear and not understood by those involved.   -3 -2 -1 0 +1 +2 +3   clear and understood by those involved.

D. **The mission and goals focus primarily on**

fleeting or inconsequential matters.   -3 -2 -1 0 +1 +2 +3   lasting, significant matters.

E. **The mission and goals were developed**

by an individual or a small influential group.   -3 -2 -1 0 +1 +2 +3   with the input of all interested parties.

F. **The mission or purpose has**

not been reviewed or revised for years.   -3 -2 -1 0 +1 +2 +3   been frequently reviewed and revised when necessary.

See next page for scoring directions.

SCORING DIRECTIONS

Relationship of You and Your Organization to Change and 21st-Century Leadership Behaviors

Directions: Add up the total number of points separately for yourself and for your organization.

80 to 126: You are an Embracer who welcomes positive change and is developing leadership behaviors for the 21st century—or you are a Pretender and have a higher view of your behaviors than reality warrants.

40 to 79: You are making positive progress on developing leadership behaviors for the future.

0 to 39: You have the potential to further develop leadership behaviors for the 21st century and need to consciously nurture them further.

0 to –39: You are a Resister to change and need to reexamine your basic premises about leadership and change.

–40 to –79: Your behaviors clearly demonstrate your resistance to change and leadership behaviors for the 21st century.

–80 to –126: You are a Denier who clings to old assumptions about the future, change, and leadership. Your beliefs are preventing you from developing effective leadership behaviors.

Fit Between You and Your Organization

Directions: For each item, count the spaces between your number and your organization's number. For example, if you gave yourself a +2 on a question and your organization a –3, then the score for that item would be a 5. Add the scores on each item.

0 to 39: There is a good fit between you and your organization. Whether you are both at the positive or the negative end of the scale, you and your organization share basic beliefs and behaviors about leadership and change.

40 to 79: You should examine the leadership behaviors to determine if the differences between you and your organization are concentrated in a few areas or spread evenly throughout the behaviors. If the differences are greatest in a few areas, realize that you and your organization are less fitted to each other in those areas, which should be monitored carefully to prevent misunderstandings or conflicts.

80 to 119: There is a high degree of misfit between you and your organization.

120+: You and your organization are completely misfitted in terms of your values, behaviors, and beliefs about leadership.

Others' Views of You and Your Organization

Directions: If you have asked individuals who know you and your organization to complete the inventory about you, compare their scores with your own. The scoring is as above, but you must pay particular attention to whether they scored you higher or lower than you scored yourself. Please keep in mind that their views are not necessarily objective or any more accurate than your own.

About the Author

Dr. Sherry Schiller is an internationally acclaimed futurist, organizational strategist, and expert on managing change. For more than 20 years, she has helped business, government, education, and nonprofit leaders understand, anticipate, and effect change.

Through consultations, speeches, workshops, and special projects, Dr. Schiller serves as a catalyst to organizations struggling to be more effective in a constantly changing environment. She helps decision makers take a more proactive stance toward the future. She provides skill-building seminars on leadership behaviors for the 21st century. Her consultations focus on results-based strategic planning, changing organizational culture, and realigning policies and practices to improve effectiveness.

Among Dr. Schiller's recent clients are such diverse groups as the U.S. Department of Agriculture, the U.S. Merit Systems Protection Board, the U.S. Department of Education, The Seeing Eye, the State of Nebraska, the Young Presidents' Organization, Gencorp, WATS Marketing, Dance/USA, The National Assembly of Local Arts Agencies, Opera America, and a host of school districts and national associations.

Dr. Schiller's work is conducted through the nonprofit 501(c)(3) organization she established in 1985, The Schiller Center. Formerly known as Countdown 2001, the Center is dedicated to assisting people and organizations in managing change. She and the Center quickly gained a national reputation for challenging established assumptions and offering fresh perspectives on organizational transformation. Dr. Schiller is a prominent keynote speaker. Her warm, lively presentation style is coupled with fresh, practical information about how to influence the future.

Before launching The Schiller Center, Dr. Schiller was the vice president of the American Center for the Quality of Work Life, where she conducted national studies on cooperative labor-management ventures and international studies on the impact of change and new technology on the workforce. Before that, she was the first national director of the Partners Program, a U.S. Department of Justice-funded project to provide community-wide support and community-service opportunities for at-risk youths. She was also a founding board member of the Center for Research and Development of Law-Related Education at the Wake Forest School of Law.

Before locating in Washington, D.C., Dr. Schiller taught at the University of Michigan as well as other universities in that state. She also taught junior high school. She received her Ph.D. from the University of Michigan, where her dissertation, a study of large-scale innovation, won the Clifford Woody Award, the university's highest scholastic honor.

For further information about Dr. Schiller and The Schiller Center, write or call the Center at 110 North Payne Street, Alexandria, VA 22314, USA. Phone: 703/684-4735, fax: 703/684-4738.